History of Portugal

Crafted by Skriuwer

At **Skriuwer**, we're more than just a team—we're a global community of people who love books. In Frisian, "Skriuwer" means "writer," and that's at the heart of what we do: creating and sharing books with readers worldwide. Wherever you are in the world, **Skriuwer** is here to inspire learning.

Frisian is one of the oldest languages in Europe, closely related to English and Dutch, and is spoken by about **500,000 people** in the province of **Friesland** (Fryslân), located in the northern Netherlands. It's the second official language of the Netherlands, but like many minority languages, Frisian faces the challenge of survival in a modern, globalized world.

We're using the money we earn to promote the Frisian language.

For more information, contact : **kontakt@skriuwer.com** (www.skriuwer.com)

Disclaimer:
The images in this book are creative reinterpretations of historical scenes. While every effort was made to accurately capture the essence of the periods depicted, some illustrations may include artistic embellishments or approximations. They are intended to evoke the atmosphere and spirit of the times rather than serve as precise historical records.

Table of Contents

Chapter 6: The Iberian Union and Decline

- 6.1 The Crisis of Succession
- 6.2 The Iberian Union
- 6.3 The Decline of the Portuguese Empire
- 6.4 The Restoration War
- 6.5 The Treaty of Lisbon

Chapter 7: The Pombaline Era

- 7.1 The Rise of the Marquis of Pombal
- 7.2 The Rebuilding of Lisbon
- 7.3 Economic and Social Reforms
- 7.4 The Expulsion of the Jesuits
- 7.5 The Legacy of Pombal

Chapter 8: The Napoleonic Wars and Brazil

- 8.1 The French Invasions of Portugal
- 8.2 The Flight of the Portuguese Court to Brazil
- 8.3 The Peninsular War
- 8.4 The Return of the Court and the Independence of Brazil
- 8.5 The Impact of Brazil's Independence on Portugal

Chapter 9: The Liberal Wars and Constitutionalism

- 9.1 The Constitutional Revolution of 1820
- 9.2 The Miguelite Wars
- 9.3 The Role of British Influence
- 9.4 The Establishment of Constitutional Monarchy
- 9.5 The Decline of Monarchical Power

Chapter 10: The First Republic

- 10.1 The Revolution of 1910
- 10.2 Political Instability and Social Change
- 10.3 Portugal in World War I
- 10.4 Economic Turmoil and Financial Crisis
- 10.5 The Downfall of the First Republic

Chapter 1

Prehistoric and Ancient Portugal

Early Human Settlement

The Iberian Peninsula, home to modern-day Portugal and Spain, boasts a rich tapestry of human history that stretches back tens of thousands of years. Archaeological evidence suggests that early human habitation in this region dates to the Upper Paleolithic period, roughly 30,000 years ago. The discovery of artifacts, cave paintings, and skeletal remains in various sites, such as the famous Altamira Cave in northern Spain, indicates that early Homo sapiens thrived in this diverse and resource-rich environment.

Paleolithic Era

During the Paleolithic era, the inhabitants of the Iberian Peninsula were primarily hunter-gatherers. They relied on the abundant flora and fauna of the region, which included large mammals such as mammoths, reindeer, and aurochs. The coastal areas and river valleys provided ample resources, allowing these early humans to develop sophisticated hunting techniques. They utilized tools made from stone, bone, and wood, some of which have been unearthed in numerous archaeological digs, revealing the ingenuity and adaptability of these early settlers.

The importance of social structures during this era can also be inferred from the burial practices observed in archaeological sites. Grave goods found alongside skeletal remains suggest a belief in an afterlife, indicating that these early humans possessed a sense of spirituality and social identity. The cave paintings found in various locations, such as the Caves of Lascaux and the Cueva de las Manos, depict scenes of hunting and ritualistic activities, further highlighting the cultural practices of these early communities.

Mesolithic and Neolithic Transitions

As the climate warmed around 10,000 years ago, the Iberian Peninsula transitioned from the Paleolithic to the Mesolithic era. This period marked significant changes in human lifestyle, as communities began to adopt more sedentary ways of living. The development of agriculture during the Neolithic period (around 6,000 BCE) further transformed these societies. The domestication of plants and animals allowed for permanent settlements and the establishment of villages, which laid the groundwork for more complex social structures.

Archaeological findings at sites such as the dolmens of Alentejo and the megalithic structures in the region reveal the architectural advancements and communal efforts of these Neolithic communities. The introduction of pottery and weaving techniques also marks a significant evolution in daily life, enabling people to store food and craft textiles, and thus enhancing their quality of life.

Cultural Interactions and Influences
The Iberian Peninsula has always been a crossroads of various cultures and peoples. The arrival of different groups, such as the Iberians, Celts, and Phoenicians, brought new influences and further shaped the social structures of the region. Interactions with these groups facilitated the exchange of ideas, technologies, and agricultural practices. For instance, the Iberians, who inhabited the eastern and southern parts of the peninsula, contributed to the development of trade networks that connected the interior with coastal regions, enhancing economic activities.

In summary, the early human settlement of the Iberian Peninsula reveals a dynamic and evolving tapestry of life, characterized by adaptability and innovation. From the hunter-gatherer societies of the Paleolithic to the agricultural communities of the Neolithic, the region's inhabitants laid the foundation for the complex civilizations that would follow. These early settlers not only shaped the landscape but also set the stage for the rich cultural heritage that defines Portugal and its place in history today.

The Influence of the Celts and Iberians
Before the Roman conquest, the Iberian Peninsula, which includes modern-day Portugal, was characterized by a rich tapestry of cultures, primarily influenced by the Iberians and Celts. These two groups, while distinct, played a crucial role in shaping the social and cultural landscape of ancient Portugal.

The Iberians
The Iberians were the indigenous inhabitants of the eastern and southern regions of the Iberian Peninsula. Archaeological evidence suggests that they settled in the area as early as the 4th millennium BCE and developed

sophisticated societies marked by advanced agricultural practices. The Iberian culture was diverse and heterogeneous, comprising various tribes with their own languages, customs, and social norms.

Iberians were primarily agrarian, cultivating crops such as wheat, barley, and olives, and they also engaged in animal husbandry. Their economy was complemented by burgeoning trade networks that extended throughout the Mediterranean, allowing for the exchange of goods such as metals, textiles, and pottery. The Iberians were skilled artisans, producing distinctive ceramics and metalwork, which reflected both functional and aesthetic considerations.

Socially, Iberian society was organized into tribes or clans, each led by chieftains or local leaders. These leaders wielded considerable power and were responsible for maintaining social order and overseeing agricultural production and trade. The Iberians practiced polytheism, revering a pantheon of gods and goddesses, which influenced their rituals and daily life. Sacred sites, often located on elevated terrain, were integral to their spiritual practices and served as communal gathering places for worship and festivals.

The Celts
The Celts began migrating to the Iberian Peninsula around the 6th century BCE, primarily from central Europe. They settled mainly in the northwestern regions, including what is now Portugal, where they merged with the local Iberian population, leading to a rich cultural syncretism. The Celtic influence introduced new social structures, customs, and technologies.

Celtic tribes were organized similarly to the Iberians, with a strong emphasis on kinship and clan relationships. They were warriors and pastoralists, relying heavily on livestock for sustenance and trade. The Celts brought with them advanced metallurgy skills, particularly in ironworking, which enhanced agricultural productivity and weaponry.

Celtic culture was rich in oral traditions, with a strong emphasis on storytelling, music, and art. They created intricate jewelry, weaponry, and pottery, often decorated with distinctive geometric patterns and motifs that reflected their beliefs and values. The Celts also had a complex religious system, worshipping nature deities and ancestors, and they performed rituals in sacred groves and hilltops.

Cultural Interactions and Syncretism

The interactions between the Iberians and Celts led to significant cultural exchange, resulting in a blended society that laid the groundwork for subsequent developments in the region. This syncretism saw the adoption of agricultural practices, religious beliefs, and artistic styles from both groups, fostering a unique cultural identity in pre-Roman Portugal.

As the Celts and Iberians coexisted, they also engaged in trade and warfare with each other, which further influenced their social dynamics. The emergence of fortified settlements, known as oppida, reflected their need for defense against external threats, including the encroaching influence of the Phoenicians and Greeks, who established trade routes along the coast.

The Roman Conquest

The Roman conquest of what is now Portugal was a significant event in the history of the Iberian Peninsula that began around the 3rd century BCE and culminated in the establishment of Roman control by the end of the 1st century BCE. This period marked the transformation of the region from a patchwork of tribal territories into a cohesive part of the vast Roman Empire, profoundly influencing its culture, society, and infrastructure.

Initially, the Iberian Peninsula was inhabited by various tribes, including the Lusitanians, Celts, and Iberians, each with their distinct customs and governance. The Romans, driven by military expansion and economic interests, began their conquest in the late 3rd century BCE, encountering fierce resistance from local tribes. The Lusitanians, in particular, led by their chieftain Viriathus, mounted a formidable guerrilla campaign against Roman forces for nearly a decade. However, the Romans' superior military tactics and resources eventually subdued these resistances.

The decisive moments of the conquest occurred during the Second Punic War (218-201 BCE), where Roman forces sought to secure their influence in the region against Carthaginian control. Following the war, the Romans intensified their military campaigns, leading to the establishment of the province of Lusitania by 27 BCE. This marked a significant shift as Roman authority was consolidated, and the integration of the local populace into the Roman system began.

The Romans employed a range of strategies to integrate Portugal into the Empire. One of the most effective was the establishment of Roman colonies, which served both as military outposts and centers for cultural assimilation. Cities such as Emerita Augusta (modern Mérida) and Pax Iulia (modern Beja) were founded during this period, acting as administrative and economic hubs that facilitated the spread of Roman culture, language, and governance. These urban centers were characterized by typical Roman architectural features, including forums, amphitheaters, baths, and temples, which not only served practical purposes but also symbolized the power and civilization of Rome.

Romanization was further promoted through the introduction of Latin as the administrative language, which gradually replaced local dialects and languages, leading to the evolution of the Portuguese language. The integration into the Roman legal system also had lasting effects on local governance, with Roman law providing a framework for justice and societal organization that would influence later Portuguese legal traditions.

Infrastructure development was another cornerstone of Roman integration. The Romans constructed an extensive network of roads, bridges, and aqueducts, facilitating trade, military movement, and communication across the region. The famous Via Augusta, which connected the far reaches of the empire, enhanced economic activity and mobility, allowing local communities to engage in trade with other parts of the Empire. This infrastructure laid the groundwork for future economic development in Portugal, fostering urban growth and agricultural productivity.

Despite the benefits of Roman rule, the integration was not without challenges. The local populace faced heavy taxation and conscription into the Roman military, leading to occasional uprisings and discontent. Nevertheless, the overall impact of Roman conquest and subsequent integration was transformative, linking Portugal to the broader Mediterranean world and embedding it within the cultural and political fabric of the Roman Empire.

As Roman control solidified, the region experienced economic prosperity, cultural enrichment, and significant demographic changes. This integration would shape the identity of Portugal for centuries to come, influencing its subsequent history through a legacy of urbanization, legal frameworks, and cultural practices that persist to this day. The Roman conquest was not merely a military endeavor; it was a profound period of change that laid the foundation for the future development of the Portuguese nation.

Romanization and Urbanization in Roman Portugal

The Roman conquest of the Iberian Peninsula fundamentally transformed the region, ushering in a period of extensive Romanization and urbanization, especially in what is now modern-day Portugal. This transformation was not merely a military endeavor; it was a comprehensive cultural and infrastructural overhaul that integrated the region into the vast network of the Roman Empire. The legacy of Romanization is evident in the archaeological remains found throughout Portugal today, as well as in the cultural and social frameworks established during this era.

Infrastructure Development

The Romans were renowned for their engineering prowess, and their influence in Portugal is most clearly illustrated through the extensive infrastructure they built. Roads were the arteries of Roman control and commerce, facilitating the movement of armies, goods, and information. The Via Augusta, which connected the far reaches of the Empire, ran through Portugal, linking important settlements and facilitating trade. The efficient road system allowed for rapid military mobilization and fostered economic growth by connecting rural areas with urban centers.

In addition to roads, the Romans constructed bridges, aqueducts, and public buildings that served both practical and symbolic purposes. The aqueduct of

Évora is a prime example, showcasing the Roman commitment to urban planning and public health. These structures not only improved the quality of life for residents but also demonstrated the might and sophistication of Roman engineering.

City Development

As part of the Romanization process, the establishment of cities was a crucial element. The Romans founded several significant towns in Portugal, many of which became vital administrative and commercial centers. Notable among these was Emerita Augusta (modern Mérida), which served as the capital of the Roman province of Lusitania. Other important cities included Olissippo (Lisbon), Scallabis (Santarém), and Bracara Augusta (Braga). Each of these cities was characterized by typical Roman urban planning: a grid layout, public forums, temples, bathhouses, and amphitheaters.

The layout of these cities reflected the Roman ideals of civic life and community. The forum, a central public space, became the heart of social, political, and economic activities. It was here that citizens gathered for markets, public speeches, and religious ceremonies, reinforcing the sense of community and belonging among the inhabitants. The construction of temples dedicated to Roman gods and the promotion of Roman cultural practices were also pivotal in solidifying the Roman influence over local populations.

Cultural Integration

Romanization in Portugal was not a one-way imposition but rather a complex process of cultural exchange. While the Romans introduced their language, laws, and customs, they also absorbed elements of local cultures. This syncretism can be seen in religious practices, art, and even local government structures, which began to incorporate Roman elements alongside indigenous traditions.

The spread of Latin, which became the dominant language, laid the groundwork for the development of the Portuguese language. Additionally, the introduction of Roman law and governance systems influenced local political structures, fostering a sense of order and civic responsibility that persisted long after the fall of the Roman Empire.

Declining Influence

The decline of Roman influence in the region was gradual, influenced by a combination of internal strife within the Empire, economic challenges, and external pressures from invading tribes. By the 5th century, the weakening of Roman authority led to the fragmentation of these urban centers, which were unable to sustain the level of infrastructure and governance established during the height of Roman power. The remnants of Roman urbanization, however, had set the stage for the emergence of new political entities and cultural identities in the Iberian Peninsula.

In conclusion, the Romanization and urbanization of Portugal were pivotal in shaping the region's historical trajectory. The infrastructure, urban planning, and cultural practices introduced during this era left a lasting legacy that influenced subsequent generations and laid the groundwork for the emergence of modern Portuguese identity. The archaeological remnants of this period continue to offer invaluable insights into the complexities of cultural integration and urban development in ancient times.

The Decline of Roman Portugal

The decline of Roman influence in what is now Portugal was a complex process influenced by a combination of internal weaknesses, external pressures, and socio-political changes. By the 3rd and 4th centuries AD, the Roman Empire was facing significant challenges that would ultimately lead to its fragmentation. The territory of present-day Portugal, known as Lusitania, experienced several factors contributing to the decline of Roman authority and the eventual transition to barbarian rule.

One of the primary internal factors was the economic strain on the Roman Empire, exacerbated by a series of crises, including inflation, military overspending, and a decline in trade. As Rome's economic structure weakened, the provinces, including Lusitania, became increasingly marginalized. The reliance on local resources and the extraction of wealth to support the imperial core in Rome left provincial regions with insufficient investment in infrastructure and local governance. This economic neglect fostered discontent among the local population, who began to question the benefits of Roman rule.

Furthermore, the social fabric of Roman Portugal began to fray under the weight of administrative inefficiency and corruption. As local elites became disenchanted with the central authority, they often sought to exert their own influence, leading to a decline in loyalty to Rome. The Roman bureaucratic system, which had once provided stability, became a burden as local leaders increasingly prioritized their interests over the interests of the Empire. This growing autonomy among local elites eroded the centralized power of Rome in the region.

Militarily, the Roman Empire faced unprecedented challenges from external forces. The 3rd century marked the beginning of significant incursions by various Germanic tribes, including the Suebi and the Vandals, who invaded the Iberian Peninsula. These tribes took advantage of Rome's weakened military presence, which had been diverted to address threats elsewhere in the Empire. The Roman legions in Lusitania were insufficient to repel these invasions, leading to a gradual loss of territory and influence. Additionally, the increasing instability of the Empire made it difficult for Rome to maintain effective defensive strategies in its provinces.

The rise of Christianity also played a role in diminishing the Roman cultural hegemony in the region. As the Christian faith spread throughout the Empire, it began to erode traditional Roman values and institutions. The growing Christian community in Lusitania often found itself at odds with Roman pagan practices, leading to social fragmentation. The establishment of Christianity as the state religion under Emperor Constantine in the early 4th century further shifted loyalties away from the Roman state to the emerging Christian Church. This shift created a new socio-political landscape that did not necessarily align with Roman interests.

By the late 4th and early 5th centuries, the culmination of these internal and external pressures led to the fragmentation of Roman authority. The establishment of the Visigothic Kingdom in the early 5th century symbolized a significant turning point for the region. The Visigoths, originally invited by Rome as foederati (allied peoples), eventually overran the Roman territories in Hispania, including Lusitania, leading to the formal end of Roman political structures.

Chapter 2

The Visigothic and Moorish Periods

The Visigothic Kingdom

The Visigothic Kingdom emerged in the early 5th century as one of the most significant powers in the Iberian Peninsula, including what is now modern-day Portugal. This period followed the decline of Roman authority in the region and set the stage for the transformation of social, political, and cultural dynamics across the area.

Initially, the Visigoths were one of several Germanic tribes that entered the Roman Empire as foederati (allied peoples) after the fall of the Western Roman Empire. They settled in the region, establishing a kingdom that expanded over the decades, reaching its zenith in the 6th century. Their influence over Portugal was marked by a series of critical developments that shaped the historical trajectory of the Iberian Peninsula.

The Visigoths brought with them a strong sense of identity, heavily influenced by their Germanic roots and the remnants of Roman culture. They established Toledo as their capital, which became a center of governance and culture, effectively radiating their influence into the areas that now comprise Portugal. The Visigothic legal system, known as the Visigothic Code (or Forum Iudicum), was a significant achievement of their monarchy. This legal framework integrated Roman legal principles with Germanic customs, facilitating governance and administration in their territories, including Portugal.

One of the hallmark features of the Visigothic era in Portugal was the integration of the local Iberian peoples into the Visigothic societal structure. The Visigoths ruled over a diverse population, including the Iberians, Celts, and Romans, and their ability to adapt and assimilate these different groups into their kingdom was paramount for stability and cohesion. The Visigothic elite intermarried with local nobility, fostering alliances that helped to consolidate their power. This blending of cultures resulted in a unique Visigothic identity that retained elements of Roman, Celtic, and indigenous Iberian traditions.

Religiously, the Visigoths initially adhered to Arian Christianity, which set them apart from the majority of the population that practiced Nicene Christianity. However, under King Reccared I, the Visigoths converted to Catholicism in 587 AD, which had profound implications for the integration of the kingdom and its subjects. This conversion facilitated the unification of the diverse religious groups across the Iberian Peninsula and helped solidify the Visigothic monarchy's legitimacy, as they aligned themselves with the dominant faith of their subjects.

Despite their achievements, the Visigothic Kingdom faced numerous challenges. Internal strife, including factionalism and power struggles among nobility, weakened their rule. The lack of a stable succession system often led to conflicts that fragmented their authority. Additionally, the rise of external threats, particularly from the Muslim forces in the early 8th century, further exacerbated the decline of the Visigothic influence.

The culmination of these pressures was marked by the Muslim invasion of the Iberian Peninsula in 711 AD, which led to the rapid collapse of Visigothic rule. The battle of Guadalete, where King Roderic met his defeat, signified the end of the Visigothic Kingdom and ushered in a new era of Islamic rule that would last for several centuries.

In conclusion, the Visigothic Kingdom played a crucial role in shaping the early medieval history of Portugal. Their governance, legal innovations, cultural integration, and religious transformation laid the groundwork for the future development of the region. The legacy of the Visigoths can still be traced through various aspects of Portuguese culture, law, and identity, reflecting a complex interplay of influences that shaped the foundations of modern Portugal.

The Moorish Invasion

The early 8th century marked a pivotal moment in the history of the Iberian Peninsula, as Muslim forces from North Africa launched a series of military campaigns that would dramatically alter the region's socio-political landscape. The invasion, often referred to as the Moorish Invasion, began in 711 AD and had profound implications for what is now modern Portugal.

Following the Islamic conquests that swept through North Africa, the Umayyad Caliphate sought to expand its territories into Europe. In 711, an army led by

Tariq ibn Ziyad crossed the Strait of Gibraltar, landing near present-day Tarifa, Spain. The rapidity and success of the Muslim forces can be attributed to several factors: the fragmentation of the Visigothic kingdom, internal strife, and the promise of religious tolerance that appealed to many inhabitants of the region.

The Visigothic kingdom, which had ruled the Iberian Peninsula since the early 5th century, was weakened by political infighting and social unrest. Infamous for their struggles over succession and governance, the ruling elite found themselves unable to mount a cohesive defense against the invaders. This internal discord allowed Muslim forces to advance rapidly into the heart of the peninsula, overcoming resistance with remarkable speed.

The conquest of Portugal began with the capture of strategic cities such as Lisbon (known as Al-Ushbuna), Sintra, and Évora. Within a few years, the majority of the Iberian Peninsula fell under Muslim control. This process of conquest did not merely involve military engagements; it also incorporated a strategy of negotiation and integration. Many local leaders and communities opted for collaboration rather than confrontation, seeking to maintain their autonomy under Muslim rule. The promise of protection, economic stability, and relative religious tolerance allowed the Moors to establish a foothold that would last for centuries.

Islamic rule profoundly influenced the cultural, social, and economic fabric of the region. The Moors introduced advanced agricultural techniques, irrigation systems, and new crops such as rice, citrus fruits, and sugarcane, which transformed the agricultural landscape of Portugal. The introduction of these practices laid the groundwork for future agricultural prosperity and played a significant role in shaping the economy.

Culturally, the Moorish presence left an indelible mark on the architecture of the region. Cities like Lisbon and Évora became vibrant centers of Islamic culture, where intricate tile work, calligraphy, and architectural styles flourished. The legacy of this period is evident in structures such as the Castle of São Jorge in Lisbon and the Almohad walls of Évora, which reflect the synthesis of Islamic and local traditions.

The Islamic period in Portugal was characterized not only by conquest but also by coexistence. Under Muslim rule, Christians and Jews often lived alongside

Muslims, contributing to a rich tapestry of cultural exchange. This era, known for its intellectual and scientific advancements, saw the preservation and translation of classical texts, fostering a unique environment of learning that influenced European thought.

Despite the relative stability and prosperity brought by the Moors, the Christian Reconquista began in the late 11th century, marking the start of a gradual and protracted effort to reclaim territories lost to Muslim control. This war for reconquest would ultimately shape the future of Portugal and herald the emergence of a unified Christian kingdom.

In summary, the Moorish Invasion was a significant event that reshaped the course of Portuguese history. It introduced new agricultural practices, cultural exchanges, and architectural innovations that left lasting impacts on the region. The complexities of this period, defined by conquest, coexistence, and cultural flourishing, set the stage for the subsequent developments in Portugal's history, leading to the establishment of a distinct national identity.

Islamic Culture and Society in Portugal

The Islamic period in Portugal, lasting from the early 8th century until the late 12th century, marked a significant transformation in the social, cultural, and scientific landscape of the Iberian Peninsula. Following the Moorish invasion in 711, a new era began, characterized by the introduction of advanced agricultural techniques, architectural innovations, and a flourishing of the arts and sciences.

Cultural Synthesis and Architectural Heritage

One of the most visible impacts of Islamic rule was the architectural legacy that remains today. The Moors introduced intricate designs characterized by geometric patterns, arabesques, and a unique use of light and space. Palaces, mosques, and fortifications were built, many of which still stand as reminders of this period. The Alhambra in Granada and the Great Mosque of Córdoba serve as iconic examples, but in Portugal, the most notable structures include the castle of Silves and the remnants of the mosque in Lisbon, later converted into the Cathedral of Lisbon.

Additionally, the Islamic influence extended beyond architecture. The introduction of new artistic styles, including ceramics and textiles, enriched the cultural fabric of the region. The tradition of azulejos, the colorful ceramic tiles that adorn many Portuguese buildings today, can be traced back to the Moorish artistic expression. These tiles not only served an aesthetic function but also played a practical role in cooling buildings in the hot climate.

Agricultural Advancements

The Islamic period also brought significant advancements in agriculture. The Moors introduced sophisticated irrigation techniques, transforming arid landscapes into fertile lands capable of supporting diverse crops. They cultivated rice, citrus fruits, and sugar cane, which were new to the Iberian Peninsula. This agricultural innovation not only improved food security but also laid the groundwork for a thriving trade economy. The introduction of these crops would eventually lead to the diversification of the Portuguese diet and agricultural practices, influencing culinary traditions that persist today.
Scientific Contributions

In addition to cultural and agricultural advancements, the Islamic period was a time of significant scientific progress. Scholars in the Muslim world were at the forefront of advancements in various fields, including mathematics, astronomy, medicine, and philosophy. Arabic numerals, which replaced the Roman numeral system, greatly facilitated trade and commerce. The concept of zero and advancements in algebra were also introduced during this time, marking a turning point in mathematical thought.

Moreover, the translation movement during the Islamic period led to the preservation and dissemination of ancient texts. Works of Greek philosophers and scientists were translated into Arabic, and later back into Latin, allowing European scholars access to knowledge that would have otherwise been lost. This intellectual activity contributed to the European Renaissance, with Portugal playing a key role as a conduit for this exchange of ideas.

Social Structure and Religious Coexistence

Islamic rule in Portugal was characterized by a relatively high degree of religious tolerance, especially in its early years. Christians, Jews, and Muslims coexisted in a society that allowed for a degree of cultural and religious exchange. This convivencia facilitated the blending of traditions, languages, and customs, which contributed to the richness of Portuguese culture. The Arabic influence is evident in the Portuguese language, where numerous words of Arabic origin can be found, particularly in areas related to agriculture, science, and everyday life.

However, as the Reconquista progressed, tensions increased, leading to the eventual expulsion or forced conversion of Muslims and Jews. The legacy of this period, however, remains deeply embedded in Portuguese society, influencing its cultural diversity and complexity.

Conclusion
The Islamic period in Portugal was a formative era that left an indelible mark on the nation's cultural, scientific, and social development. The fusion of Islamic and Iberian traditions laid the foundation for a unique cultural identity that continues to be a source of pride for contemporary Portugal. The advancements in agriculture, architecture, and science during this time not only enriched the Portuguese heritage but also contributed to the broader European intellectual landscape, underscoring the importance of this era in understanding Portugal's historical trajectory.

The Christian Reconquest

The Christian Reconquest, or Reconquista, was a pivotal period in the history of the Iberian Peninsula, marked by the efforts of Christian kingdoms to reclaim territory that had fallen under Muslim control since the early 8th century. In Portugal, this movement played a crucial role in shaping the nation's identity, culture, and political landscape.

Following the Muslim invasion in 711 AD, much of the Iberian Peninsula, including what is now Portugal, came under the control of the Umayyad Caliphate. Over the next few centuries, the region saw a blend of cultures, but the Christian kingdoms in the north began to rally against Muslim rule. The Reconquista was not merely a military campaign; it was also a deep-seated ideological struggle fueled by religious fervor and a desire to restore Christian dominion over the lands that had been lost.

The early stages of the Reconquista in Portugal were characterized by a series of skirmishes and battles. One of the most significant figures during this period was Count Vímara Peres, who led the Christian forces to reclaim territory in the early 9th century. His victories laid the groundwork for the establishment of the County of Portugal under the Kingdom of León. The Christian forces, often composed of local nobles and their followers, capitalized on the internal divisions within the Muslim territories, exploiting moments of weakness to launch their offensives.

The Christian Reconquest gained significant momentum in the 12th century under the leadership of Afonso Henriques, who would later become the first King of Portugal. Afonso's ambitions were fueled by both military strategy and the theological justification of holy war. His campaigns against Muslim strongholds, such as the decisive Battle of Ourique in 1139, were framed as divinely sanctioned endeavors. Following his victory, Afonso declared himself king, marking the official recognition of Portugal as an independent kingdom.

Afonso's reign was characterized by aggressive territorial expansion. He systematically targeted key cities and fortresses, including Lisbon in 1147, which fell to the combined forces of Afonso and a contingent of northern European crusaders en route to the Holy Land. The capture of Lisbon was not only a strategic victory; it also symbolized the reclamation of an important urban center that would become a pivotal hub of Christian power in the region.

The Reconquista was not without its challenges. The Muslim forces regrouped and counterattacked, leading to fluctuating control over various territories. Internal strife among Christian factions also complicated the efforts, as regional rivalries occasionally undermined the collective goal of reclaiming the peninsula. However, with the backing of the Church and the growing sense of a unified Christian identity, the momentum gradually shifted in favor of the Christian kingdoms.

By the late 12th century, the Reconquista in Portugal had reached a crucial juncture. The Treaty of Zamorra in 1143 formalized the independence of Portugal from León, while subsequent campaigns saw the consolidation of territory and the establishment of the borders of modern Portugal. The Reconquista ended in the Iberian Peninsula with the fall of Granada in 1492, but its effects lingered, deeply embedding notions of religious identity and cultural unity into the Portuguese psyche.

In summary, the Christian Reconquest was a transformative period in the history of Portugal. It was marked by military endeavors, religious zeal, and the eventual establishment of an independent kingdom that would lay the foundations for Portugal's future as a maritime and colonial power. The legacy of this era continues to resonate in Portugal's cultural and national identity today, reflecting the complexities of its historical journey through conflict and reconciliation.

The Formation of the County of Portugal

The formation of the County of Portugal in the 12th century represents a pivotal moment in the historical trajectory of the Iberian Peninsula, particularly in the context of the Reconquista—a prolonged military campaign by Christian kingdoms aimed at reclaiming territory occupied by Muslim forces. The intricate interplay of political, social, and military factors during this period laid the groundwork for the eventual establishment of an independent Portuguese state.

In the early 11th century, the Iberian Peninsula was fragmented into various territories controlled by Muslim and Christian leaders. The Christian kingdoms of León and Castile were engaged in a series of conflicts with Muslim territories, seeking to expand their dominions and reclaim lost lands. It was within this context that the County of Portugal emerged as both a military and territorial entity. The initial formation can be traced back to the establishment of the County of Portucale in 868, which was officially recognized as a vassal state of the Kingdom of León. This nascent county was strategically located along the Douro River, benefiting from fertile lands and a robust trade network.

The key figure in the emergence of the County of Portugal was Count Henry of Portugal, a nobleman of Burgundian descent. In the early 12th century, Count Henry played a crucial role in the military campaigns against the Muslim-held territories in the south. His marriage to Teresa of León, the illegitimate daughter of King Alfonso VI of León and Castile, further solidified his status and laid the groundwork for the eventual establishment of Portuguese autonomy. Following Count Henry's death in 1112, his son Afonso Henriques ascended to leadership, marking a significant turning point in the history of the region.

Afonso Henriques, later known as Afonso I of Portugal, was a formidable military leader. He capitalized on the ongoing Reconquista, leading campaigns that expanded the territory of the County of Portugal. His military successes included the capture of Lisbon in 1147, a significant event that not only showcased his military prowess but also strengthened the county's position within the Christian kingdoms of the Iberian Peninsula. The successful sieges and conquests helped to galvanize support for Afonso's aspirations for independence.

The pivotal moment came in 1139 when Afonso declared himself king, a proclamation that was met with mixed reactions among the neighboring kingdoms. The recognition of Afonso's claim to kingship was solidified by the Treaty of Zamorra in 1143, where he received formal acknowledgment from King Alfonso VII of León and Castile. This treaty not only recognized Afonso as king but also delineated the borders between the newly established Kingdom of Portugal and the existing territories of León and Castile. This act of recognition was crucial, as it provided legitimacy to the Kingdom of Portugal and affirmed its sovereignty.

The formation of the County of Portugal was significantly influenced by the broader context of the Reconquista. The military and religious motivations behind the Reconquista fostered a sense of identity among the Christian kingdoms, enabling Afonso Henriques to rally support and resources for his campaigns. The integration of religious fervor with political ambition catalyzed the desire for autonomy, allowing the County of Portugal to assert itself against the backdrop of competing kingdoms.

In conclusion, the emergence of the County of Portugal from the Reconquista was a complex process shaped by strategic military leadership, dynastic alliances, and the broader geopolitical landscape of the Iberian Peninsula. Afonso Henriques's ability to unify Christian forces and capitalize on the fragmentation of Muslim rule ultimately led to the establishment of an independent and enduring Portuguese identity, setting the stage for the future evolution of the nation.

Chapter 3

The Birth of Portugal

The Treaty of Zamora

The Treaty of Zamora, signed in 1143, marked a pivotal moment in the history of Portugal, serving as the official acknowledgment of its independence from the Kingdom of León. This treaty not only solidified the emergence of Portugal as a discrete political entity but also laid the groundwork for the future development of the Portuguese monarchy and its territorial aspirations.

Context of the Treaty

In the early 12th century, the Iberian Peninsula was characterized by the fragmentation of power among various Christian kingdoms and the ongoing struggle to reclaim territory from Muslim rule. The Kingdom of León, one of the most powerful Christian states of the time, had exerted considerable influence over much of the northwest Iberian Peninsula, including the region that would become Portugal. The rise of Afonso Henriques, the Count of Portugal, was instrumental in changing this dynamic. Following his military successes against the Moors and his ambitions to expand his realm, Afonso declared himself King of Portugal in 1139 after a significant victory at the Battle of Ourique.

However, Afonso's claim to kingship was contested by King Alfonso VII of León and Castile, who viewed Portugal as a part of his realm. This led to a power struggle, culminating in a series of military confrontations and diplomatic negotiations. The conflict highlighted the tensions between the burgeoning identity of the Portuguese and the established authority of León, setting the stage for the eventual treaty.

The Negotiations

As the hostilities continued, both sides recognized the need for a resolution that would prevent further bloodshed. In 1143, a diplomatic meeting took place in Zamora, a city in the Kingdom of León. This meeting was crucial as it brought together representatives from both kingdoms to negotiate the terms of recognition for Portugal's sovereignty. The negotiations were fraught with challenges, as both parties had to balance their desire for territorial integrity with the need for stability in the region.

Ultimately, the Treaty of Zamora recognized Afonso Henriques as the King of Portugal, marking the first formal acknowledgment of Portugal as an independent kingdom. This treaty provided a framework for the relationship between Portugal and León, establishing the borders and delineating the extent of their respective territories.

Significance of the Treaty

The Treaty of Zamora was significant for several reasons. First and foremost, it legitimized Afonso Henriques' claims to the throne and established Portugal as a sovereign state, separate from León. This recognition was crucial for consolidating power and fostering national identity among the Portuguese people.

Furthermore, the treaty allowed Afonso to focus on internal governance and further territorial expansion. With the formal backing of León, he could consolidate his rule and strengthen the foundations of the Portuguese monarchy. This included fortifying cities, developing agricultural lands, and promoting trade, which would contribute to the economic stability of the nascent kingdom.

The Treaty of Zamora also had lasting implications for Portuguese and Spanish relations. By recognizing Portugal's independence, the treaty set a precedent for the future political landscape of the Iberian Peninsula, where negotiations and treaties became essential tools for managing territorial disputes. It established a framework for diplomacy that would influence relations between the two kingdoms for centuries.

Conclusion

In conclusion, the Treaty of Zamora in 1143 was a landmark event that not only marked Portugal's independence but also laid the foundations for its future as a unified kingdom. This critical moment in history signified the triumph of Afonso Henriques and the aspirations of the Portuguese people for self-determination. The treaty not only shaped the political landscape of the Iberian Peninsula but also fostered a sense of national identity that continues to resonate in Portugal's cultural heritage today.

The Reign of Afonso I

Afonso I, known as Afonso Henriques, was a pivotal figure in the establishment of the Portuguese monarchy and the foundation of Portugal as a distinct political entity in the 12th century. Born around 1109, Afonso was the son of Count Henry of Portugal and Teresa of León, the illegitimate daughter of King Alfonso VI of León and Castile. His lineage positioned him within the context of the Iberian power struggles of the time, where the influence of both Christian kingdoms and Muslim territories was profoundly felt.

Afonso's reign began in earnest after he became count of Portugal in 1139, following his declaration of independence from León. This bold move was both a political and military assertion, as he sought to establish a separate identity for his territory. His coronation as king in 1139 was significant not only for the act itself but for its implications in the broader context of Iberian politics. Afonso's claim to kingship was initially met with skepticism, as he was still technically a vassal of León. However, his military successes and ability to consolidate power within his realm lent credibility to his authority.

One of the defining features of Afonso Henriques's reign was his relentless military campaign against the Muslim-held territories in the south. He strategically aimed at expanding his domain through a series of conquests, most notably the capture of Lisbon in 1147, aided by a contingent of Northern European crusaders. This victory was crucial, as it not only secured a significant coastal city for Portugal but also symbolized the broader Christian Reconquista movement against Islamic rule in the Iberian Peninsula. Afonso's ability to rally support from diverse groups, including Crusaders, underscored his political acumen and military prowess.

Afonso's reign was characterized by a strong centralization of power. He initiated policies that strengthened the monarchy and reduced the influence of local nobility, who had traditionally held significant power in the region. Through the issuance of charters to towns and the establishment of legal frameworks, Afonso sought to promote loyalty to the crown and create a sense of national identity among his subjects. This was particularly important in a time when regional loyalties often transcended allegiance to the monarchy. Afonso's efforts laid the groundwork for a more cohesive state, which would evolve into modern Portugal.

The establishment of the Portuguese monarchy under Afonso I also involved significant interactions with the Catholic Church. Afonso sought the church's endorsement to legitimize his reign, navigating the complex dynamics of ecclesiastical power. His relationship with the papacy was instrumental; in 1179, Pope Alexander III recognized Afonso as king, which further solidified his authority and marked an important step in the international recognition of Portugal as a sovereign entity.

Moreover, Afonso Henriques set a precedent for the role of the monarchy in Portuguese governance. His reign established a model of kingship that combined military strength with diplomatic savvy, which would influence his successors. The consolidation of power, territorial expansion, and the establishment of a robust monarchy during his reign were pivotal in shaping Portugal's future trajectory.

In summary, Afonso I's reign was marked by military conquests, strategic alliances, and the consolidation of royal authority, laying the foundational stones for the Portuguese monarchy. His legacy is a testament to the complexities of state-building in medieval Europe, characterized by the interplay of power, religion, and identity in the formation of what would become a significant European nation. Afonso Henriques stands as a critical figure not only in Portuguese history but also in the broader narrative of the Reconquista and the emergence of nation-states in the medieval period.

Expansion and Consolidation

The expansion and consolidation of Portugal during the early medieval period reflect a dynamic and transformative phase in the nation's history, characterized by territorial conquests, diplomatic maneuvering, and the establishment of a cohesive national identity. This period, particularly under the rule of Afonso I (Afonso Henriques) and his successors, was critical in shaping the future of the Portuguese monarchy and its territorial ambitions.

After the Treaty of Zamora in 1143, which recognized Portugal's independence from León, Afonso I embarked on a series of military campaigns aimed at expanding his kingdom's borders southward into the Muslim-held territories of the Iberian Peninsula. This initiative was not merely a quest for land; it was also driven by the desire to solidify Portugal's status as an independent power in the face of its larger and more influential neighbors, such as León and Castile.

Afonso's early conquests included the capture of Lisbon in 1147, which became a pivotal moment in Portuguese history. This strategic port city not only served as a vital economic hub but also helped to establish Portugal's maritime capabilities, facilitating trade and exploration.

The consolidation of territory was accompanied by efforts to integrate the newly acquired lands into the fabric of the nascent kingdom. This process involved the resettlement of populations, the establishment of fortified towns (cidades), and the promotion of agriculture and trade. The king granted lands to his loyal knights and vassals, fostering a feudal system that would provide military support and loyalty in exchange for land. The creation of these fiefdoms helped establish a network of loyal noble families who would play crucial roles in the governance of the expanding kingdom.

Afonso I's reign was characterized by a strong military ethos, embodying the ideals of chivalry and the Christian crusading spirit. The Reconquista was not only a religious campaign but also a means of unifying the population under a common cause. Afonso's appeals to the Church for support were instrumental in garnering resources and legitimacy for his conquests. His relationship with the Papacy allowed for the formal recognition of his title as King of Portugal, reinforcing his authority and the legitimacy of his rule.

Following Afonso I, his successors continued the pattern of expansion and consolidation. Notably, King Sancho I and King Afonso II further pressed southward, capturing significant territories such as the Algarve region. The establishment of the County of Portugal as a distinct entity was crucial in fostering a sense of national identity among its inhabitants. The kings also focused on fortifying existing cities and building new ones, which served as administrative and military centers, enhancing the kingdom's control over its territories.

The consolidation of power was not limited to military conquests; it also involved diplomatic engagements with neighboring kingdoms. The Portuguese monarchs sought to navigate the complex political landscape of the Iberian Peninsula by forming strategic alliances and marriages with prominent noble families. These alliances helped to stabilize the kingdom and mitigate threats from more powerful neighbors.

In conclusion, the early Portuguese kings' expansion and consolidation efforts were marked by a combination of military prowess, strategic governance, and diplomatic acumen. By integrating newly acquired territories and fostering a sense of national identity, they laid the groundwork for a unified and resilient kingdom. This period not only set the stage for future territorial ambitions but also established the cultural and political foundations that would characterize Portugal for centuries to come. The legacy of these early efforts continues to resonate in the modern Portuguese state, reflecting the enduring significance of this formative era in the nation's history.

The Role of the Church in Early Portuguese State-Building

The Catholic Church played a pivotal role in the formation and consolidation of the early Portuguese state, intertwining religious authority with emerging political power. From the establishment of the County of Portugal in the 12th century to the solidification of the monarchy under Afonso I, the Church was a crucial ally in legitimizing and supporting the nascent Portuguese state.

Religious Legitimacy and Monarchical Authority

The Church provided the necessary religious legitimacy that early Portuguese rulers required. Afonso Henriques, the first King of Portugal, sought the endorsement of the Church to strengthen his claim to the throne and unify the diverse territories under his control. By aligning himself with the Church, Afonso I not only validated his rule but also gained the loyalty of the populace, many of whom were staunchly Catholic. The Church's blessing was instrumental in portraying Afonso as a divinely appointed leader, a notion that helped solidify his authority and justify military campaigns against both Muslim and Christian adversaries.

The Reconquista and the Church's Influence

The backdrop of the Reconquista—an ongoing effort to reclaim territories in the Iberian Peninsula from Muslim control—further intertwined the Church and the state. The Catholic Church actively supported these military endeavors, viewing the Reconquista as a holy war. Papal bulls granted indulgences to those who fought in these campaigns, encouraging participation and framing the conflict as not only a political struggle but also a religious obligation. This fervor helped galvanize support for Afonso I and his successors, as victories in battle were celebrated in the context of religious triumph.

The establishment of monasteries and churches throughout the reconquered territories played a dual role. They served as religious centers that spread Christianity but also acted as administrative hubs that facilitated the consolidation of power. Monastic communities were often granted land in return for their spiritual services, and this land became crucial for the economic support of the monarchy.

Administrative Functions and Economic Influence

The Church's influence extended beyond religious and military realms into the administrative and economic spheres of early Portuguese society. Bishops and abbots often held significant political power, acting as key advisors to the king and wielding considerable influence over local governance. Their roles in managing land and resources made them indispensable allies in the early state-building process. Additionally, the Church's vast landholdings contributed significantly to the economy, as agricultural production supported both the clergy and the monarchy.

The Church also provided education and literacy, which were predominantly concentrated in monastic institutions during this period. By promoting knowledge and culture, the Church played a pivotal role in shaping the identity of the early Portuguese state. This educational influence was crucial in fostering a literate clergy and administrative class, essential for effective governance and the documentation of laws and royal decrees.

Cultural and Social Integration

Beyond its political and economic roles, the Church was instrumental in promoting cultural integration within the diverse populations of early Portugal. The Church's doctrine and liturgy often transcended ethnic and linguistic barriers, promoting a shared identity among the various groups within the kingdom. This cultural assimilation was vital, particularly in regions with mixed populations where Christian and Muslim influences coexisted.

As the Catholic Church fostered a sense of national identity through shared religious practices, it helped to forge a cohesive social fabric that was essential for the stability of the early Portuguese state. The church's festivals, rituals, and community gatherings became focal points for local populations, reinforcing the unity and identity of the emerging nation.

Relations with Neighboring Kingdoms

The formative years of Portugal's history were marked by complex and often contentious interactions with neighboring kingdoms, particularly Castile and León. The geographical proximity and shared cultural heritage between these Iberian kingdoms fostered both cooperation and conflict, shaping the political landscape of the region from the 12th to the 14th centuries.

After the establishment of the County of Portugal in the late 11th century, the region was caught in the midst of the Reconquista, a centuries-long campaign by Christian kingdoms to reclaim territory from Muslim rule. In this context, the relationship between Portugal and its larger neighbors became increasingly significant. Afonso I, also known as Afonso Henriques, the first king of Portugal, was central to the early diplomatic and military maneuvers that defined these interactions. He sought to expand his territory while negotiating alliances that would bolster Portugal's position against both Muslim forces and rival Christian kingdoms.

In 1139, Afonso declared himself king, and his reign was characterized by both military conquests and strategic diplomacy. One notable interaction was with the Kingdom of León, which was initially a rival. In 1143, the Treaty of Zamorra was signed between Afonso I and León's King Alfonso VII. This treaty recognized the independence of Portugal, although it did so under the condition that Afonso would not expand further into León's territory. This diplomatic success laid the groundwork for Portugal's recognition as a legitimate kingdom, although tensions remained as both kingdoms vied for influence in the region.

The dynamics of power shifted frequently as the kingdoms of Castile, León, and Portugal engaged in a series of alliances and rivalries. The marriage arrangements between royal families were common strategies for solidifying peace or asserting claims. For instance, Afonso II of Portugal (1185-1211) married the daughter of Alfonso IX of León, reflecting how personal relationships intertwined with political ambitions. However, these alliances often proved fragile. The centuries that followed were marked by intermittent warfare as territorial ambitions clashed, particularly during the reign of Afonso III of Portugal, who sought to expand his kingdom into lands held by León and Castile.

The 13th century saw the consolidation of the Portuguese crown under Afonso III, who effectively utilized both military campaigns and diplomatic negotiations to strengthen Portugal's borders. His reign marked a significant era where Portugal began to assert its identity distinct from Castile and León. The capture of key cities such as Faro and Silves was pivotal, as it expanded Portuguese influence along the southern coast and increased tensions with its neighbors.

As time progressed, political and military interactions evolved. The rise of the Kingdom of Castile, particularly under Ferdinand III, posed new challenges for Portugal. The Treaty of Badajoz in 1267, which defined the borders between Portugal and Castile, was an attempt to establish a lasting peace, yet it became clear that the ambitions of both kingdoms would continue to provoke conflict in the future.

By the late 14th century, the emergence of the Aviz dynasty and the subsequent crisis of succession further complicated relations. The 1383-1385 Crisis, marked by the struggle for the Portuguese crown, resulted in the Battle of Aljubarrota (1385), where Portuguese forces, under John I, defeated the Castilian army. This decisive victory not only solidified John I's claim to the throne but also reinforced Portugal's independence from Castile, setting the stage for its future as a sovereign nation.

In summary, the relations between Portugal and its neighboring kingdoms of Castile and León were characterized by a blend of diplomatic negotiations, strategic marriages, and military confrontations. These interactions were crucial in shaping the identity and boundaries of early Portugal, ultimately contributing to its emergence as a distinct and independent kingdom in the Iberian Peninsula.

Chapter 4

The Age of Discovery

The Rise of the Portuguese Maritime Empire

In the 15th century, Portugal emerged as a preeminent maritime power, setting the stage for an era of exploration and conquest that would reshape the world. The country's rise as a maritime empire was not an overnight phenomenon; rather, it was the result of a confluence of geographic, political, economic, and cultural factors.

Portugal's advantageous geographic position along the western edge of the Iberian Peninsula made it ideally suited for maritime endeavors. Bordered by the Atlantic Ocean, the Portuguese coastline facilitated navigation and fishing. The natural harbors along the coast served as safe havens for the burgeoning fleet of ships that would undertake exploratory voyages. As European nations looked beyond their borders, Portugal's strategic location provided them with direct access to the Atlantic and beyond.

The Age of Exploration was significantly influenced by the evolving political landscape within Portugal itself. In the early 15th century, Portugal was unified under the rule of the Aviz dynasty, particularly under King John I and his successors. This period fostered a sense of national identity and aspiration for expansion. The Portuguese monarchy recognized the potential of overseas exploration not only as a means to gain wealth but also as a way to spread Christianity, particularly in response to the Reconquista, which had recently concluded in 1492 with the fall of Granada.

A critical figure in this endeavor was Prince Henry the Navigator, a royal patron of exploration who initiated the first stages of Portugal's maritime expansion. Although he did not personally embark on voyages, he established a navigation school in Sagres that became a hub for learning and innovation in navigation and shipbuilding. Under his guidance, Portuguese mariners developed new navigational techniques, improved ship designs (notably the caravel), and utilized advanced tools such as the astrolabe, which allowed sailors to determine their latitude at sea with greater accuracy.

By the mid-15th century, Portuguese explorers began to venture along the West African coast. The desire to find a sea route to the riches of the East, particularly the lucrative spice markets of India and the Far East, drove these expeditions. Explorers like Gil Eanes successfully navigated the Cape Bojador in 1434, breaking the psychological barrier that had previously deterred mariners from venturing further south. Subsequent voyages led to the discovery of the Azores and the Madeira archipelago, further extending Portugal's territorial claims and influence.

The pinnacle of Portugal's maritime expansion came with the voyages of Vasco da Gama, who, in 1498, became the first European to reach India by sea. This monumental achievement opened up direct trade routes to Asia, allowing Portugal to establish a vast trading network. Following da Gama's success, other explorers, including Afonso de Albuquerque, expanded Portuguese influence in the Indian Ocean, capturing key ports and establishing a presence in places like Goa and Malacca.

The establishment of these trade routes not only enriched the Portuguese crown but also led to significant cultural exchanges. Portuguese traders brought back exotic goods such as spices, silks, and precious metals, which transformed the European economy and fueled the rise of a merchant class. The influx of wealth from the East enabled further investment in maritime technology and exploration, perpetuating a cycle of expansion.

Thus, the rise of the Portuguese maritime empire in the 15th century can be attributed to a combination of geographic advantages, royal ambition, technological innovation, and a relentless pursuit of trade and exploration. This period laid the groundwork for Portugal to become one of the foremost maritime powers of the early modern world, ultimately leading to its vast empire that spanned continents. The ramifications of this maritime ascendancy would resonate for centuries, influencing global trade patterns, cultural exchanges, and the course of history itself.

Prince Henry the Navigator

Prince Henry the Navigator, born in 1394, is often heralded as a pivotal figure in the Age of Discovery, a period marked by extensive exploration that reshaped global geopolitics and economies. Although he never personally sailed on the voyages he sponsored, his contributions to maritime exploration and the advancement of navigation were profound and far-reaching.

Henry was the third son of King John I of Portugal and his English wife, Philippa of Lancaster. He inherited an intense curiosity and a desire to expand Portugal's influence beyond its borders. His early interests in exploration were sparked by the desire to find new trade routes and to spread Christianity, particularly against the backdrop of the Reconquista, which sought to reclaim land from Muslim control in the Iberian Peninsula.

In 1415, Henry played a crucial role in the capture of Ceuta, a North African city that served as a strategic gateway for trade and military expeditions. This victory not only marked the beginning of Portugal's expansion into Africa but also ignited Henry's passion for exploration. Establishing a base in Ceuta allowed him to further contemplate and organize more extensive maritime ventures.

Recognizing the need for improved navigation techniques, Henry established a school of navigation at Sagres, at the southwestern tip of Portugal. While the exact nature and extent of this institution are subjects of scholarly debate, it is widely accepted that it attracted some of the best navigators, cartographers, and shipbuilders of the time. Under his patronage, significant advancements were made, including the development of the caravel, a new type of ship that was faster and more maneuverable, capable of sailing against the wind and exploring uncharted waters.

Henry's focus on cartography and navigation was instrumental in developing accurate maps of the African coastline and beyond. He sponsored numerous expeditions along the West African coast, leading to the discovery of the Madeira Islands and the Azores. These voyages were crucial not only for geographical knowledge but also for establishing trade routes that would later facilitate the transatlantic slave trade and the spice trade, which were economically vital to Portugal.

As a devout Christian, Henry also had a missionary zeal. He envisioned not only material wealth from exploration but also the spread of Christianity. His expeditions often sought to establish contacts with African kingdoms and convert their leaders and peoples to Christianity, seeing this as both a moral obligation and a means to expand Portuguese influence.

Henry's commitment to exploration had lasting impacts on Portugal and the world. By promoting navigational advancements and sponsoring voyages, he laid the groundwork for later explorers, including Vasco da Gama and Ferdinand Magellan. His efforts initiated a wave of exploration that ultimately led to the establishment of a vast Portuguese Empire stretching across Africa, Asia, and Brazil.

Despite his significant contributions, it is important to acknowledge that the consequences of these explorations were complex. While they led to the exchange of goods and ideas, they also initiated periods of colonization and exploitation that would have lasting ramifications for indigenous populations.

In summary, Prince Henry the Navigator's legacy is multifaceted. His visionary approach to exploration and navigation not only propelled Portugal to the forefront of maritime endeavors in the 15th century but also set in motion a series of events that would profoundly alter the course of global history. His ambition and foresight contributed to the emergence of an era characterized by exploration, trade, and cultural exchange, the effects of which continue to resonate in the modern world.

Key Voyages and Explorations

The Age of Discovery, spanning the 15th and 16th centuries, marked a pivotal era in global history, characterized by remarkable maritime exploration, particularly by Portugal. Among the most notable figures of this period was Vasco da Gama, whose expeditions not only transformed the Portuguese economy but also redefined global trade routes and cultural exchanges.

Vasco da Gama's journey to India, which commenced in 1497, was a landmark event that solidified Portugal's position as a dominant maritime power. Commissioned by King Manuel I, da Gama was tasked with finding a sea route to India that would enable Portugal to access the lucrative spice trade, which until then was controlled by Middle Eastern and Asian intermediaries. This mission was crucial for Portugal, as spices such as pepper, cinnamon, and cloves were highly sought after in Europe, driving both economic and exploratory ambitions.

Departing from Lisbon, da Gama's fleet consisted of four ships. The expedition first made its way down the African coast, navigating treacherous waters and dealing with the complexities of local politics and trade. Notably, da Gama stopped at the Cape Verde Islands and then continued to the Kingdom of Mali, where he engaged in trade, further enhancing the expedition's prospects. Ultimately, his journey led him to the Cape of Good Hope, a significant milestone that marked the passage from the Atlantic to the Indian Ocean.

Upon reaching the Indian subcontinent in May 1498, da Gama landed at Calicut, on the southwestern coast of India. This initial encounter was marked by cultural exchanges as well as tension, as local rulers were cautious of the Europeans' intentions. Da Gama faced challenges in establishing a foothold, but after securing a favorable trade agreement, he returned to Portugal in 1499, bringing back spices and a wealth of knowledge about the Indian market.

The implications of da Gama's voyage were monumental. It opened up a direct maritime route to India, enabling Portugal to bypass traditional overland trade routes controlled by Islamic empires and city-states. This not only allowed Portugal to monopolize the spice trade but also led to the establishment of a series of trading posts along the Indian coastline, including those at Cochin and Malacca, further expanding Portuguese influence in the East.

Following da Gama, subsequent explorers such as Pedro Álvares Cabral continued to chart new territories, leading to the discovery of Brazil in 1500. Cabral's expedition also reinforced Portugal's presence in the Indian Ocean, as he engaged with the region's trade networks and established further outposts. The establishment of these trade routes fostered a global exchange of goods, ideas, and cultures, fundamentally altering the course of history.

The Portuguese exploration efforts during this era were not without consequences. The establishment of trade routes led to significant cultural exchanges but also had devastating impacts on indigenous populations, including the spread of diseases and the imposition of colonial rule. The wealth generated from these explorations fueled the rise of the Portuguese Empire, allowing it to become a formidable power in global affairs.

In summary, the key voyages and explorations of the 15th and 16th centuries, particularly those led by Vasco da Gama, were instrumental in shaping the trajectory of not only Portugal but also the world at large. These expeditions marked the beginning of an age where European powers sought to expand their influence across continents, laying the groundwork for globalization and the interconnected world we know today.

The Establishment of Trade Routes

The establishment of trade routes by Portugal during the Age of Discovery marked a pivotal moment in global commerce and cultural exchange. This period, spanning the late 15th to the early 17th centuries, was characterized by Portugal's aggressive maritime exploration, leading to the creation of a vast trading network that connected Europe with Africa, Asia, and the Americas.

Portugal's quest for trade routes began with the motivation to access the lucrative spice markets of the East. Spices such as pepper, cinnamon, and nutmeg were highly prized in Europe, not only for their use in culinary practices but also for their value in preserving food and their perceived medicinal properties. The traditional overland routes were controlled by powerful intermediaries including the Ottoman Empire and various Arab traders, which made direct access to these spices difficult and expensive.

The initiative was spearheaded by figures such as Prince Henry the Navigator, who, although he did not sail himself, was instrumental in promoting exploration. His establishment of a navigation school in Sagres, along with state-sponsored expeditions along the West African coast, laid the groundwork for future maritime endeavors. By the 1440s, Portuguese explorers had reached the Senegal River, marking the beginning of a systematic exploration of the African coastline.

The real breakthrough came with Vasco da Gama's voyage to India in 1497. By navigating around the Cape of Good Hope, Da Gama opened the first direct maritime route to Asia. His journey was not merely a singular achievement; it was the culmination of decades of navigational advancements. Upon reaching Calicut, Da Gama established trade relations, securing agreements that allowed for the Portuguese to trade in spices directly, thus bypassing the previous overland routes.

Following Da Gama, the establishment of trade routes expanded rapidly. The Portuguese set up trading posts and forts along key coastal areas, creating a network that included locations in Africa (such as Elmina and Luanda), India (notably Goa), and later, the spice islands of Indonesia. These posts acted as hubs for trade, protection for Portuguese merchants, and strategic points for naval operations. The fortified city of Goa became the cornerstone of Portuguese power in Asia, serving as the administrative center for their eastern possessions.

In addition to spices, the Portuguese trade network facilitated the exchange of other goods, including gold, ivory, and sugar, particularly from their colonies in Brazil. The establishment of sugar plantations in Brazil, using enslaved African labor, became a significant economic driver for the Portuguese Empire. This sugar trade not only enriched Portugal but also had profound implications for the transatlantic slave trade, as millions of Africans were forcibly transported to work in the colonies.

The Portuguese employed a variety of methods to secure their trade routes. They formed alliances with local rulers, often employing a strategy of diplomacy and marriage to gain favor and access. Moreover, they adapted to local customs and practices, which allowed for smoother operations in foreign territories. However, this expansion was not without conflict; the Portuguese frequently clashed with other European powers, particularly the Dutch and the English, who sought to undermine their monopoly on the spice trade.

The establishment of these global trade routes transformed not only Portugal's economy but also the nature of global trade itself. Portugal's innovative maritime strategies and their ability to integrate diverse markets into a cohesive trading network laid the groundwork for the modern globalization we observe today. The network not only enriched Portugal but also facilitated cultural exchanges, influencing cuisines, languages, and societies across continents. Ultimately, the legacy of these trade routes is a testament to Portugal's role as a pioneer of maritime exploration and global trade in the early modern era.

The Impact on Indigenous Populations

The Age of Discovery marked an era of unprecedented exploration, during which Portugal emerged as a formidable maritime power. This expansion was not merely a quest for new trading routes but also led to profound and often devastating impacts on the indigenous populations of the territories they encountered. The Portuguese were among the first Europeans to establish extensive contacts with various cultures across Africa, Asia, and South America, and the consequences of these interactions were multifaceted.

Cultural Assimilation and Syncretism

In many regions, the arrival of Portuguese explorers and settlers initiated a complex process of cultural exchange. In places like Brazil, the Portuguese imposed their language, religion, and customs on indigenous groups. However, this was not a one-sided process; indigenous peoples also influenced Portuguese culture, leading to a unique syncretism. For example, the blending of indigenous and Portuguese religious practices gave rise to new forms of worship, as seen in the incorporation of African and Native American elements into Catholic rituals. This cultural fusion enriched the Portuguese identity, creating a diverse tapestry that reflected the realities of colonization.

Economic Exploitation and the Slave Trade

One of the most significant and tragic impacts of Portuguese exploration was the onset of economic exploitation, which often translated into brutal systems of labor extraction. The Portuguese established lucrative sugar plantations in Brazil, which relied heavily on the forced labor of indigenous peoples and, increasingly, African slaves. The introduction of the transatlantic slave trade during the 16th century had catastrophic effects on both indigenous populations and African societies. Many indigenous communities were decimated through forced labor, violence, and the introduction of European diseases to which they had no immunity. This led to dramatic demographic shifts, with some indigenous groups facing near extinction.

Land Dispossession and Social Disruption

The arrival of the Portuguese often resulted in the dispossession of indigenous lands. As settlers claimed territories for agriculture and resource extraction, native populations were forcibly removed from their ancestral lands. This displacement led to significant social disruption, as traditional ways of life were dismantled. Indigenous communities faced not only the loss of land but also the erosion of their social structures, cultural practices, and languages. In many cases, indigenous peoples were relegated to the status of marginalized laborers in their own territories, further alienating them from their heritage.

Resistance and Adaptation

Despite the overwhelming forces of colonization, indigenous populations did not passively accept their fate. Many groups resisted Portuguese encroachments through armed conflict, diplomacy, or by adapting their strategies for survival. The Guarani people in Brazil, for instance, engaged in armed resistance against Portuguese settlers, while others sought alliances with the Portuguese to gain protection against rival tribes. This resistance showcased the resilience and agency of indigenous peoples, highlighting their role in shaping the colonial narrative.

Lasting Consequences

The impact of Portuguese exploration on indigenous populations has had long-lasting ramifications. The legacy of colonization is still felt in contemporary society, as many indigenous peoples continue to struggle for recognition, rights, and reparations. The historical narratives surrounding colonization have led to ongoing debates about identity, heritage, and justice in post-colonial contexts.

Chapter 5

The Height of the Portuguese Empire

Portugal as a Global Power

The 16th century marked an unparalleled era for Portugal, often referred to as the Age of Discovery, during which the nation emerged as a formidable maritime and colonial power. This period was characterized by extensive exploration, territorial expansion, and the establishment of a global empire that spanned several continents. The factors contributing to Portugal's ascendancy as a global power during this time were multifaceted, involving technological advancements, strategic leadership, and the burgeoning demand for trade.

At the heart of Portugal's rise was its innovative maritime technology and navigational expertise. The development of the caravel, a small, highly maneuverable ship, allowed Portuguese explorers to traverse the treacherous waters of the Atlantic and beyond. This vessel, coupled with advancements in cartography and navigation techniques, enabled sailors to embark on long voyages with greater confidence and precision. Pioneers such as Vasco da Gama opened new sea routes, most notably the sea passage to India around the Cape of Good Hope in 1498, which was pivotal in establishing direct trade links with the Indian subcontinent.

The Portuguese Empire's territorial holdings reached their zenith in the 16th century, expanding across Africa, Asia, and South America. Notable territories included parts of modern-day Brazil, Angola, Mozambique, Goa, and territories in Japan and China. The Treaty of Tordesillas in 1494, brokered by the papacy, divided newly discovered lands between Spain and Portugal, granting the latter substantial rights over vast swathes of the globe. This diplomatic maneuvering was instrumental in securing Portuguese dominance in the spice trade, which was immensely lucrative and sought after in European markets.

The establishment of a global trading network also underpinned Portugal's power. The Portuguese did not merely seek territorial conquests; they aimed to create a vast economic empire built on trade. The spice trade, in particular, became the backbone of the Portuguese economy, with merchants establishing trading posts and forts in strategic locations along the coasts of Africa and Asia. Cities such as Lisbon transformed into bustling commercial hubs, serving as the epicenter for the exchange of goods, cultures, and ideas.

Cultural exchange was a significant aspect of Portugal's global influence. Portuguese explorers and traders interacted with diverse cultures and societies, leading to a blending of traditions, languages, and religions. The introduction of Christianity was often a part of the colonial agenda, with missionaries accompanying explorers to convert indigenous populations. This cultural syncretism enriched Portuguese society, as seen in the influences on language, cuisine, and religious practices stemming from encounters with African, Asian, and Indigenous cultures.

However, the zenith of Portuguese power was not without its challenges. The vast empire was difficult to manage, and the competition with other emerging European powers, particularly Spain, England, and the Netherlands, began to strain resources. The reliance on maritime trade also made Portugal vulnerable to piracy and naval conflicts, which would later contribute to its decline.

In conclusion, the 16th century epitomized Portugal's momentous rise as a global power, characterized by an expansive empire, thriving trade networks, and rich cultural exchanges. This period laid the groundwork for Portugal's enduring legacy in world history, with its influence still resonating in various aspects of global culture today. The combination of maritime innovation, strategic territorial acquisitions, and the establishment of a global trading network not only defined this era but also set a precedent for future explorations and imperial pursuits by European powers.

The Colonial Administration

The colonial administration of Portugal during its imperial zenith in the 16th and 17th centuries was characterized by a complex interplay of governance structures, economic policies, and cultural exchanges that shaped the nature of its vast overseas territories. At its height, the Portuguese Empire spanned several continents, including Africa, Asia, and South America, making it one of the first global empires in history. This expansive reach necessitated a sophisticated approach to administration that balanced local governance with the overarching authority of the Crown.

Centralized Authority and Local Governance

The Portuguese Crown established a centralized system for managing its colonial possessions, delegating authority to a network of governors, viceroys, and administrators who oversaw the day-to-day operations of the colonies. The most notable of these was the Viceroy of India, who governed the Portuguese territories in Asia from Goa and was responsible for protecting trade routes, maintaining order, and managing relations with local rulers and other colonial powers.

Local governance often took on a semi-autonomous nature, especially in regions where indigenous governance structures were already established. For instance, in Brazil, local elites known as "donatários" were granted extensive powers to govern specific territories, encouraging the integration of indigenous customs and practices into the colonial administration. While this facilitated local compliance and governance, it also led to significant variations in administration across different regions of the empire.

Economic Exploitation and Trade Regulation

Economically, the Portuguese colonial administration was heavily focused on the extraction of resources and the establishment of lucrative trade networks. The crown implemented a mercantilist policy designed to maximize revenue from its colonies. This included the control of key commodities, such as sugar from Brazil and spices from India and the Spice Islands. The administration regulated trade through a system of charters and monopolies, granting exclusive rights to certain merchants and companies, such as the Portuguese East India Company. The administration also established trading posts and forts along critical trade routes, such as those along the coasts of Africa and Asia, to secure trade interests and protect against rival European powers. These fortified trading posts served as both commercial hubs and military outposts, exemplifying the dual role of the Portuguese colonial administration in promoting commerce while ensuring the security of its interests.

Cultural Exchange and Missionary Activity

The colonial administration of Portugal was not solely a function of governance and trade; it was also deeply entwined with cultural exchange and missionary work. The Portuguese Crown, influenced by the Catholic Church, viewed its colonial expansion as an opportunity for religious conversion. Missionaries, particularly the Jesuits, played a vital role in establishing schools, churches, and hospitals in the colonies, aiming to convert indigenous populations to Christianity.

This missionary activity often resulted in a syncretism of cultures, where local traditions blended with Portuguese and Christian elements. In Brazil, for example, African and indigenous cultures intermingled with Portuguese customs, giving rise to unique cultural expressions in music, dance, and religious practices that continue to influence Brazilian culture today.

Challenges and Adaptations

Despite its initial success, the Portuguese colonial administration faced numerous challenges, including competition from other European powers, internal dissent, and difficulties in communication and resource allocation across vast distances. The reliance on local intermediaries often led to corruption and inefficiency, and the sheer scale of the empire made it difficult to maintain effective control over distant territories.

In response, Portugal adapted its administrative practices, incorporating local knowledge and customs into governance. This flexibility allowed for a degree of resilience, enabling the empire to withstand pressures from rival powers and internal strife for centuries.

In conclusion, the colonial administration of Portugal was marked by a combination of centralized authority, economic exploitation, cultural exchange, and adaptability. These elements not only facilitated the governance of a vast empire but also left a lasting impact on the regions it encompassed, shaping their cultures, economies, and societies in profound ways that continue to resonate today.

The Spice Trade and Economic Impact

The spice trade was a cornerstone of Portugal's economic prosperity during the 16th century, marking a period when the nation ascended to global prominence through its pioneering maritime explorations. As the demand for exotic spices surged in Europe, particularly in the wake of the Black Death, spices such as pepper, cloves, nutmeg, and cinnamon became highly sought after not only for culinary purposes but also for their medicinal properties and as symbols of wealth and status. Portugal, leveraging its strategic position and maritime innovations, emerged as a principal player in this lucrative trade.

The key to Portugal's success lay in its ability to establish direct sea routes to the spice-rich islands of the East Indies, particularly the Maluku Islands, also known as the Spice Islands. This was spearheaded by explorers such as Vasco da Gama, whose landmark voyage to India in 1498 opened the sea route to Asia. Following Gama, other explorers ventured further into the Indian Ocean, paving the way for the establishment of trading posts and colonies. The Portuguese captured critical coastal ports in Africa, India, and eventually the Spice Islands, enabling them to control the flow of spices into Europe and eliminate the middlemen who had previously dominated the trade.

The economic impact of the spice trade on Portugal was profound. The influx of wealth from spices translated into significant financial resources for the Portuguese Crown, which used these funds to expand its naval capabilities, fortify its colonies, and engage in further exploration. The establishment of the Estado da Índia, a colonial administration, allowed for systematic governance and protection of Portuguese interests in Asia, ensuring that profits from the spice trade were maximized and secured against competitors, including the Dutch and English, who sought to usurp Portuguese dominance.

Notably, the spice trade also facilitated the development of a complex network of trade routes that interconnected Europe, Africa, and Asia. As Portuguese ships ventured into these regions, they not only transported spices but also brought back other valuable goods, including precious metals, textiles, and sugar. This trade diversification allowed Portugal to strengthen its economy, as merchants and investors saw opportunities to profit from a burgeoning global market.

The economic benefits of the spice trade extended beyond mere wealth accumulation; it also stimulated various sectors within Portugal. The rise of mercantilism during this period led to increased state intervention in the economy, fostering a commercial culture that prioritized trade and maritime expansion. Port cities such as Lisbon thrived as bustling centers of commerce, attracting merchants, craftsmen, and laborers, which in turn contributed to urbanization and infrastructural development.

However, the spice trade did not come without challenges. The wealth it generated led to internal conflicts and rivalries, both among Portuguese merchants and with foreign powers seeking to enter the trade. The Dutch, in particular, became formidable competitors, leading to a series of conflicts known as the Dutch-Portuguese War. These tensions highlighted the precariousness of Portugal's position in the global trade network and foreshadowed the eventual decline of Portuguese supremacy in the spice trade.

In conclusion, the spice trade was a catalyst for Portugal's economic expansion during the Age of Discovery. It enriched the nation, transformed its economy, and positioned it as a central player in global trade. The legacy of this trade can still be felt today, not only in the historical narrative of Portugal but also in the culinary traditions that reflect the enduring influence of spices across cultures. The wealth generated by the spice trade laid the groundwork for Portugal's future endeavors, shaping its identity as a maritime power and leaving an indelible mark on world history.

Cultural Exchange and Syncretism

The Portuguese Empire, at its height in the 16th and 17th centuries, was one of the earliest and most enduring colonial enterprises in history. Its vast global reach, spanning continents from Africa and Asia to the Americas, facilitated a profound cultural exchange and syncretism that shaped both the metropole and its colonies. This process was marked by the blending of indigenous cultures with Portuguese traditions, resulting in unique cultural identities that continue to resonate in contemporary societies.

One of the most significant aspects of cultural exchange was in the realm of language. The Portuguese language, enriched by the influences of various indigenous tongues, became a vehicle for communication and cultural transmission. In Brazil, for instance, indigenous words were incorporated into the Portuguese lexicon, particularly in the fields of flora, fauna, and local customs. Words like "tapioca," derived from the Tupi language, and "piranha," from the Guarani, illustrate how indigenous languages contributed to the Portuguese vocabulary. This linguistic syncretism not only reflects the merging of cultures but also signifies a broader acceptance and recognition of the diverse identities within the empire.

Religious syncretism also played a crucial role in the cultural exchange between Portugal and its colonies. The Portuguese Crown, motivated by a desire to spread Catholicism, often employed missionaries to convert indigenous populations. However, this imposition of religion did not occur in isolation. In many cases, local beliefs and practices were integrated into the Catholic framework. For instance, in Brazil, elements of African spirituality were blended with Catholic rituals, resulting in unique religious practices such as Candomblé and Umbanda. This fusion of faiths created new cultural expressions that celebrated both African heritage and Catholic traditions, demonstrating the resilience and adaptability of indigenous cultures in the face of colonial domination.

The arts also flourished through this exchange, leading to the emergence of hybrid styles that reflected the confluence of different cultural influences. In architecture, the Manueline style, characterized by intricate ornamentation, emerged in Portugal and later influenced colonial structures in Brazil and Africa. Similarly, the introduction of Portuguese baroque elements in churches and public buildings in colonial territories created a distinct architectural language that signified both the power of the Crown and the adaptation to local contexts.

Culinary traditions provide another vivid example of cultural syncretism. The Portuguese introduced new ingredients and cooking techniques to their colonies, which were then combined with local culinary practices. In Brazil, for instance, the use of ingredients like cassava (manioc) and tropical fruits, alongside Portuguese recipes, gave rise to a unique gastronomy, exemplified by dishes like feijoada—a hearty stew that has become a national dish, blending African, indigenous, and Portuguese influences.

Furthermore, trade routes established by the Portuguese facilitated an exchange of goods that went beyond mere commodities. The spice trade, for example, not only brought wealth to Portugal but also introduced new flavors and ingredients that were integrated into Portuguese cooking. This exchange was reciprocal, as local products like sugar and tobacco transformed Portuguese markets and lifestyles, fostering a deeper connection between the colonizers and the colonized.

In summary, cultural exchange and syncretism between Portugal and its colonies were pivotal in shaping the identities of both Portuguese society and the societies within its empire. The blending of languages, religions, artistic expressions, and culinary traditions created rich, hybrid cultures that reflect a complex history of interaction. This syncretism not only enriched the cultural tapestry of Portugal and its colonies but also laid the groundwork for ongoing dialogues about identity, heritage, and globalization in the modern world. The legacy of this intricate cultural exchange continues to inform and inspire contemporary discussions about the interconnectedness of societies across the globe.

Challenges and Conflicts

The height of the Portuguese Empire in the 16th and early 17th centuries was marked not only by its vast territorial holdings and global influence but also by numerous challenges and conflicts that threatened its stability and longevity. These challenges arose from both internal dynamics within the empire and external pressures from rival powers and the complexities of global trade.

Internal Challenges

One of the key internal challenges faced by the Portuguese Empire was the difficulty of governing a vast and diverse array of territories that spanned across continents. The empire included colonies in Africa, Asia, and South America, each with different cultures, languages, and social structures. This diversity often led to administrative inefficiencies and difficulties in enforcing imperial policies. The distance between the metropole and the colonies compounded these issues, making it challenging for the Portuguese Crown to maintain effective control and oversight.

Additionally, the empire struggled with social unrest and resistance from colonized peoples. In various regions, local populations resisted Portuguese rule, leading to uprisings and conflicts. For instance, in India, the Portuguese faced significant pushback from local rulers and rival European powers, such as the Dutch and the British, who were expanding their own colonial ambitions. The resistance undermined Portuguese authority and stretched military resources thin.

The empire was also plagued by internal dissent and factionalism. The nobility and powerful merchant classes often vied for influence, leading to political infighting that weakened the central authority of the Crown. Such divisions were exacerbated by the increasing wealth disparity between the elite and the working classes, leading to social tensions that could destabilize the empire from within.

External Pressures

Externally, the Portuguese Empire faced significant competition from other emerging European powers. The late 16th century saw the rise of the Dutch Republic and England as formidable maritime forces. The Dutch were particularly aggressive in their pursuit of trade routes and colonies, directly challenging Portuguese monopolies in the spice trade and other lucrative markets. The Dutch-Portuguese War (1602-1663) exemplified this competition, resulting in significant losses for Portugal, including the capture of key territories in Asia.

Additionally, the Spanish Habsburgs, who ruled Portugal during the Iberian Union from 1580 to 1640, imposed their own political agendas, which often conflicted with Portuguese interests. The association with Spain brought Portugal into the broader conflicts of the Habsburg dynasty, including the Thirty Years' War. Many Portuguese resented Spanish dominance, leading to a growing sense of nationalism and ultimately contributing to the Restoration War, which sought to reclaim Portuguese independence.

Economic challenges also loomed large on the horizon. The reliance on the spice trade made the economy vulnerable to fluctuations in demand and competition. The discovery of alternative trade routes and sources in the East by other European powers diminished the profitability of Portuguese trade and strained the imperial economy. As the empire expanded, the costs associated with military protection, administration, and infrastructure development became burdensome, leading to financial difficulties.

In conclusion, the challenges and conflicts faced by the Portuguese Empire during its height were multifaceted, encompassing internal governance issues, social unrest, external competition, and economic vulnerabilities. These pressures not only tested the resilience of the empire but also set the stage for its eventual decline. Understanding these dynamics provides valuable insights into the complexities of imperial governance and the delicate balance required to maintain power in a rapidly changing global landscape. The interplay of these internal and external factors ultimately shaped the trajectory of Portugal's imperial ambitions and its historical legacy.

Chapter 6

The Iberian Union and Decline

The Crisis of Succession

The Crisis of Succession in Portugal, which culminated in the Iberian Union under Philip II of Spain, was a pivotal moment in the history of the Portuguese monarchy and the broader Iberian Peninsula. This crisis was rooted in a complex interplay of dynastic tensions, political maneuvering, and the changing landscape of European power dynamics in the late 16th century.

The immediate trigger of the crisis lay in the death of King Sebastian I of Portugal in 1578 at the Battle of Alcácer-Quibir, where he led an ill-fated expedition against Morocco. Sebastian's demise was particularly significant because he left no direct heirs, creating a power vacuum in the Portuguese monarchy. This absence of a clear successor sparked a fierce contest for the throne, as various claimants emerged, each with their own ambitions and backing. Among the most prominent was Cardinal Henry, Sebastian's uncle, who ascended to the throne as Henry I. However, his reign was short-lived; he passed away in 1580 without producing an heir, further deepening the monarchy's instability.

The situation was exacerbated by the political landscape of the time. Portugal's status as a prominent maritime power had drawn the attention of neighboring Spain, which was under the rule of King Philip II. Philip, a grandson of Isabella of Castile and Ferdinand of Aragon, had a vested interest in Portuguese affairs due to his own claims through his mother, who was a Portuguese princess. As the Spanish crown was also embroiled in conflicts across Europe, including wars with France and the Netherlands, the prospect of uniting Portugal and Spain under one crown became increasingly appealing to Philip.

As the Portuguese nobility struggled to consolidate power amidst the chaos, Philip II seized the opportunity. In 1580, he laid claim to the Portuguese throne, arguing that he was the rightful heir due to his familial ties. This claim was met with resistance from a faction of Portuguese nobles who supported António, Prior of Crato, a distant cousin of Sebastian who had declared himself king. The ensuing conflict, known as the Portuguese succession crisis, led to a civil war as loyalists of both Philip and António vied for control.

The conflict culminated in the decisive Battle of Alcântara in August 1580. Philip's forces, consisting of seasoned Spanish troops, defeated the forces loyal to António. Following this victory, Philip II was proclaimed King of Portugal, formally initiating the Iberian Union. This union lasted for sixty years, during which Portugal retained its own laws, customs, and colonial possessions, albeit under the overarching rule of the Spanish crown.

While the Iberian Union promised stability, it was fraught with challenges. Many Portuguese resented the loss of their independence and the dominance of Spanish rule, leading to subsequent resistance movements. The union also strained Portugal's international relations, particularly with England and France, as they viewed the consolidation of power in the Iberian Peninsula with suspicion.

In conclusion, the Crisis of Succession in Portugal was a complex and turbulent period marked by the interplay of dynastic ambition, political intrigue, and military conflict. The resolution of this crisis through the Iberian Union under Philip II of Spain not only altered the trajectory of Portuguese history but also set the stage for future struggles over national identity and sovereignty that would resonate through subsequent centuries. The legacy of this union continues to inform Portugal's historical narrative, reflecting the enduring tension between independence and external authority.

The Iberian Union (1580-1640)

The Iberian Union, a significant event in the history of Portugal, marked a period of dynastic union between Portugal and Spain from 1580 to 1640. This union was driven by a combination of succession crises, political maneuvering, and the geopolitical landscape of the Iberian Peninsula, resulting in profound implications for both nations.

The roots of the Iberian Union can be traced back to the death of King Sebastian I of Portugal in 1578 at the Battle of Alcácer Quibir, where he led a disastrous military campaign in Morocco. King Sebastian's death, without an heir, created a power vacuum and a succession crisis in Portugal. His great-uncle, Cardinal Henry, ascended to the throne but ruled for only a short time before his own death in 1580. This left Portugal in a precarious position, as multiple claimants emerged, notably Philip II of Spain, who was the son of Isabella of Portugal (Sebastian's aunt) and Charles V, Holy Roman Emperor.

Philip II, seeking to consolidate his power and control over the Iberian Peninsula, claimed the Portuguese throne, asserting that he had legitimate rights through his maternal lineage. In 1580, he managed to assert his claim after a brief civil war, which pitted his forces against those loyal to Portuguese nobility who sought to maintain the independence of the kingdom. The war culminated in the Battle of Alcântara, where Philip's forces secured victory, leading to his proclamation as King of Portugal.

The Iberian Union did not imply the complete annexation of Portugal into Spain; rather, Portugal retained its legal status as a separate kingdom, albeit under the Habsburg crown. Philip II and his successors ruled both kingdoms through a dual monarchy. However, this arrangement was fraught with tension as many Portuguese resented Spanish dominance and perceived their sovereignty as compromised. The imposition of Spanish customs, taxes, and military obligations further fueled discontent among the Portuguese populace.

During this period, Portugal's global empire faced new challenges. The Spanish crown diverted resources to other imperial pursuits, which resulted in neglect of Portuguese colonies. The economic repercussions of this neglect were significant, as the spice trade – a vital component of Portugal's economy – suffered. Additionally, the growing influence of Spanish bureaucratic practices clashed with Portuguese traditions, leading to administrative inefficiencies and widespread dissatisfaction.

Resistance against Spanish rule was not limited to the nobility; it also found expression among various social classes. The Portuguese clergy, particularly, were vocal in their opposition to the union, as they feared that Spanish rule would undermine the autonomy of the Church in Portugal. The growing resentment culminated in social unrest and unrest within the clergy, which further destabilized the union's legitimacy.

The final years of the Iberian Union were marked by increasing resistance, culminating in the Restoration War that began in 1640. The Portuguese nobility, motivated by a desire for independence and fueled by the perceived failures of

Spanish rule, orchestrated a coup d'état that resulted in the overthrow of the Spanish governor. On December 1, 1640, Portugal declared its independence, leading to a protracted conflict with Spain, which sought to reassert control.

The Iberian Union ultimately ended in 1640 with the Treaty of Lisbon in 1668, which formally recognized Portugal's sovereignty. The union profoundly impacted the national identity of Portugal, fostering a sense of unity among its people in the face of foreign rule and setting the stage for the emergence of a distinct Portuguese national consciousness that would persist in the centuries to follow. The period of the Iberian Union serves as a critical chapter in the history of Portugal, highlighting themes of sovereignty, identity, and resistance that resonate throughout its subsequent history.

The Decline of the Portuguese Empire

The decline of the Portuguese Empire, which reached its zenith in the 16th century, can be attributed to a multitude of factors that collectively led to the weakening of Portugal's global dominance. These factors are complex and interwoven, encompassing economic, political, social, and military dimensions.

Economic Challenges: At the height of its empire, Portugal's economy was heavily reliant on the spice trade and other commodities extracted from its colonies. However, as the 17th century progressed, competition intensified from other European powers, particularly the Dutch and the English, who began to dominate the spice trade routes and establish their own colonies. The Dutch, in particular, captured significant Portuguese territories in the East Indies, severely impacting Portugal's economic foundations. Furthermore, the discovery of alternative trade routes and sources for spices diminished Portugal's monopoly, leading to a decline in revenues from its overseas possessions.

Political Instability: The political landscape in Portugal underwent significant upheaval during the 17th century. The Iberian Union (1580-1640), which merged the crowns of Portugal and Spain under Philip II, created discontent among the Portuguese populace. Many viewed this union as a loss of sovereignty, leading to a decline in national pride and identity. The centralized Spanish authority often disregarded Portuguese interests, resulting in resentment that fueled nationalist sentiments. This dissatisfaction culminated in the Restoration War (1640-1654), where Portugal successfully regained its independence, but the struggle left the nation politically weakened and economically strained.

Military Setbacks: The military capabilities of the Portuguese Empire faced serious challenges, particularly in the face of growing external threats. The Dutch-Portuguese War (1602-1663) saw the Dutch systematically attacking Portuguese trade routes and colonies, resulting in significant territorial losses. Furthermore, the rise of Britain as a naval power and its subsequent conflicts with Portugal further eroded the latter's military standing. The inability to effectively defend its colonies and trade routes meant that Portugal could not maintain its global influence.

Colonial Overextension: As the Portuguese Empire expanded, it became increasingly difficult to manage the vast and diverse territories spread across continents. The administrative challenges of governing such an extensive empire strained resources and led to inefficiencies. Many colonies suffered from neglect, and local discontent grew as the Portuguese government struggled to address the needs and aspirations of diverse populations. This overextension made it difficult for Portugal to respond effectively to internal revolts and external threats.

Social and Cultural Factors: The social fabric of Portugal began to change, as the wealth from colonies did not translate into widespread prosperity for the Portuguese people. Instead, the wealth often accumulated in the hands of a small elite, leading to social tensions and economic disparities. The decline in the prestige of the Portuguese monarchy and nobility, coupled with the rising influence of the bourgeoisie, contributed to a changing political landscape that undermined traditional power structures.

The Impact of Decolonization: The eventual wave of decolonization that swept through the world in the mid-20th century further highlighted the decline of the Portuguese Empire. The Carnation Revolution in 1974 marked a significant turning point, as Portugal abruptly relinquished its colonial possessions in Africa and Asia, leading to the rapid dismantling of its empire. This loss not only diminished Portugal's global influence but also resulted in a significant economic and demographic shift.

In conclusion, the decline of the Portuguese Empire was a multifaceted process influenced by economic competition, political instability, military setbacks, colonial overextension, and social changes. The repercussions of this decline reshaped Portugal's identity and its role on the global stage, setting the foundation for the modern nation it is today.

The Restoration War

The Restoration War (1640-1654) was a pivotal conflict that marked Portugal's struggle to regain its independence from Spanish rule, which had lasted 60 years under the Iberian Union. This war was not merely a military campaign but a significant national uprising fueled by a deep-seated desire for autonomy and identity, reflecting the broader themes of nationalism and sovereignty that would resonate through European history.

Historical Context

The roots of the Restoration War can be traced back to the dynastic crisis following the death of King Henry of Portugal in 1580. With no clear heir, the Portuguese crown was claimed by Philip II of Spain, leading to the annexation of Portugal into the Spanish Empire. This union was met with resistance from many Portuguese nobles and commoners alike, who felt that their unique identity, language, and traditions were being overshadowed by Spanish culture and governance. Over the years, resentment against Spanish rule grew, fueled by heavy taxation, military conscription, and the suppression of Portuguese customs.

The Spark of Rebellion

The turning point came on December 1, 1640, when a group of Portuguese nobles, including important figures such as the Duke of Braganza, conspired to overthrow the Spanish government. This date is celebrated as Portugal's Restoration Day. The coup was successful; the conspirators captured the royal palace in Lisbon and proclaimed John IV, the Duke of Braganza, as king. John IV's ascension was not merely a change in leadership; it symbolized the restoration of the Portuguese monarchy and the revival of national pride.

The War Effort

Following the successful coup, the newly established Portuguese government had to prepare for the inevitable Spanish response. The Spanish Crown viewed the rebellion as a direct challenge to its authority and swiftly mobilized an army to crush the uprising. The ensuing conflict saw several key battles, including the Battle of Montijo in 1644 and the Battle of Alcântara in 1640, where Portuguese forces managed to achieve significant victories, bolstered by local support and a fervent desire for independence.

Despite initial successes, the war was far from straightforward. The Portuguese faced challenges, such as a lack of resources and the need to unify various factions within the country. However, the leadership of John IV and the military prowess of commanders like Afonso de Albuquerques galvanized the Portuguese forces. Additionally, the Portuguese navy played a crucial role in securing coastal areas and disrupting Spanish supply lines.

International Dynamics

The Restoration War was not an isolated conflict. It occurred within a broader context of European politics, including the Thirty Years' War, which was ongoing during this period. Portugal sought alliances with France and England, who were both interested in curbing Spanish power. This international dimension added complexity to the war, as both sides sought to gain external support for their causes.

Conclusion of the War

The Restoration War culminated with the Treaty of The Hague in 1661, which formally recognized Portugal's independence and ended hostilities. The outcome of the war restored Portugal as a sovereign nation, allowing it to reclaim its identity and re-establish its empire overseas. The Restoration War not only marked a significant moment in Portuguese history but also set a precedent for future independence movements within Europe and beyond.

In essence, the Restoration War was a testament to the resilience and determination of the Portuguese people. It reinforced national identity and pride, laying the groundwork for the future development of a modern Portuguese state. The legacy of this conflict continues to be celebrated in Portugal, symbolizing the enduring spirit of a nation that fought to reclaim its sovereignty and cultural heritage.

The Treaty of Lisbon

The Treaty of Lisbon, signed on February 13, 1668, marked a pivotal moment in the history of Portugal. It not only signified the formal recognition of Portuguese independence from Spanish rule but also reflected the complex political, social, and economic dynamics that characterized the Iberian Peninsula during the 17th century. This treaty concluded a period of crisis and conflict that had begun with the Iberian Union in 1580 when Portugal was absorbed into the Spanish Empire under Philip II.

Historical Background

The Iberian Union, which lasted for nearly 60 years, was a union of the crowns of Spain and Portugal, prompted by a dynastic crisis following the death of King Sebastian of Portugal. His death without an heir led to a succession dispute, which Philip II of Spain, a grandson of King Manuel I of Portugal through his mother, claimed. This union was met with resistance from many Portuguese who viewed it as a loss of sovereignty and national identity. Over time, discontent grew among the Portuguese populace, exacerbated by heavy taxation, military conscription, and Spain's involvement in costly wars that drained Portuguese resources.

In the early 1640s, the desire for independence culminated in a revolt against Spanish rule, known as the Restoration War. This conflict, which began in 1640, was driven by the aspirations of the Portuguese nobility and common people alike, who yearned for autonomy and reinstatement of their monarchy. Leadership under John IV, who was proclaimed king in 1640, galvanized support for the independence movement.

The Restoration War

The Restoration War waged for nearly three decades, characterized by military engagements and shifting alliances. The Portuguese forces, despite being outnumbered at times, employed guerrilla tactics and leveraged their knowledge of the local terrain to mount significant resistance against the Spanish forces. The war was not only a military struggle but also a cultural renaissance that sought to revive and reclaim Portuguese identity, language, and customs. By the late 1660s, both Spain and Portugal had sustained heavy losses. The economic toll and the public dissatisfaction with continued conflict led to negotiations. The Spanish government, recognizing the untenable situation, sought a resolution that would restore peace and stabilize the region.

The Treaty of Lisbon

Negotiations culminated in the Treaty of Lisbon, which was signed in the Portuguese capital. The treaty recognized the sovereignty of Portugal and formally ended the Iberian Union. It established the mutual agreement of both nations, affirming that Portugal was to be governed independently, free from Spanish interference. This was not merely a diplomatic victory but a profound statement of national identity and pride, reinvigorating the spirit of the Portuguese people.

The treaty also included provisions for the return of certain territories and the establishment of trade relations, which were crucial for the recovering Portuguese economy. While the treaty did not resolve all issues—tensions and disputes continued in the years following—it laid the groundwork for a renewed sense of national identity.

The Legacy of the Treaty of Lisbon

The Treaty of Lisbon is celebrated in Portuguese history as a cornerstone of national independence. It not only marked the end of foreign domination but also allowed Portugal to embark on a path of recovery and development. The restoration of the monarchy under John IV initiated a period of cultural flourishing and economic revitalization, setting the stage for Portugal's later engagements in global affairs, including its role in the Age of Discovery.

In contemporary discussions, the Treaty of Lisbon serves as a reminder of the resilience of national identity in the face of oppression and the enduring human desire for self-determination. It remains a significant symbol of Portugal's journey through tumultuous times and a testament to the complex interplay of power, identity, and sovereignty in European history.

Chapter 7

The Pombaline Era

The Rise of the Marquis of Pombal

The Marquis of Pombal, born Sebastião José de Carvalho e Melo in 1699, emerged as one of the most notable figures in Portuguese history, particularly during the mid-18th century. His ascent to power was marked by a combination of political acumen, economic foresight, and a commitment to modernization that would leave a lasting impact on Portugal.

Pombal's early life laid the foundation for his future influence. He was born into a noble family in the city of Lisbon and received a solid education, which included studies in law, philosophy, and literature. His initial foray into politics began in the early 1720s when he served in various diplomatic roles, including a significant appointment as the Portuguese ambassador to Great Britain. This experience equipped him with a nuanced understanding of international relations and the complexities of European politics.

Pombal's true rise to power began in 1750 when he was appointed Minister of State by King Joseph I. The timing was crucial; Portugal was in the midst of a significant transformation. The 1755 Lisbon earthquake had devastated the city, resulting in massive loss of life and property. The king, recognizing the need for effective leadership during this crisis, turned to Pombal, who would prove instrumental in the city's reconstruction and recovery.

Upon assuming power, Pombal embarked on an ambitious program of reforms aimed at revitalizing the Portuguese economy and modernizing its administrative structures. He recognized that the country was lagging behind its European counterparts, particularly in terms of infrastructure, education, and the economy. Pombal implemented policies that encouraged commerce, including the promotion of agriculture and industry. He initiated significant infrastructural projects, such as the rebuilding of Lisbon with wider streets and better public services, which not only addressed the immediate needs following the earthquake but also laid the groundwork for a more modern urban environment.

Pombal's influence extended beyond economic reforms; he was also a staunch advocate for Enlightenment ideals. He sought to curb the power of the Catholic Church, which had substantial control over Portuguese society and politics. In 1759, he expelled the Jesuits from Portugal, an act that was both a bold political maneuver and a reflection of his commitment to secular governance and educational reform. By reducing the Church's influence, Pombal aimed to promote rational thought and scientific advancement, aligning Portugal with the broader trends of the Enlightenment occurring across Europe.

His reforms were not without controversy. While many praised his vision and effectiveness, others viewed him as a tyrant. Pombal's authoritarian methods, including the use of censorship and political repression against dissenters, led to significant opposition. His administration was characterized by a centralized control that allowed him to implement reforms swiftly but also fostered resentment among the aristocracy and those who favored traditional power structures.

Despite the challenges, Pombal's legacy is one of modernization and resilience. His vision for a stronger, more prosperous Portugal was evident in the advances made during his tenure. He fostered a sense of national identity and pride, positioning Portugal as a progressive nation in an era of change. By the time he fell from favor in 1777, following the death of King Joseph I, Pombal had irrevocably altered the landscape of Portuguese society, economy, and governance.

In summary, the rise of the Marquis of Pombal marked a significant turning point in Portuguese history. His leadership during a time of crisis and his commitment to reform established him as a pivotal figure, whose influence shaped the course of Portugal long after his departure from power.

The Rebuilding of Lisbon

On November 1, 1755, Lisbon was struck by a catastrophic earthquake that, along with the subsequent tsunami and fires, devastated the city and resulted in the deaths of tens of thousands of people. This disaster, one of the most significant in European history, not only caused immense human suffering but also posed profound challenges for the Portuguese government, society, and economy. The reconstruction of Lisbon emerged as a pivotal moment in Portugal's history, showcasing advancements in urban planning and architectural philosophy that would influence future city developments across Europe.

In the immediate aftermath of the earthquake, the sheer scale of destruction was overwhelming. Approximately 85% of Lisbon's buildings were damaged or destroyed, including critical infrastructure such as churches, schools, and hospitals. The social fabric of the city was torn apart, with many left homeless and in desperate need of support. The devastation prompted a national crisis, leading to widespread calls for reform and modernization of the city.

The Marquis of Pombal, Sebastião José de Carvalho e Melo, emerged as the key figure in the reconstruction efforts. Appointed as the Secretary of State for Foreign Affairs and War, Pombal took on the responsibility of leading the recovery with a decisive and pragmatic approach. His vision for a rebuilt Lisbon was not merely to restore what had been lost but to create a modern city that could withstand future disasters. Under his guidance, the reconstruction was characterized by innovative urban planning principles, emphasizing order, functionality, and aesthetics.

Pombal's efforts led to the establishment of the Baixa Pombalina, an entirely new downtown area built on a grid plan that was revolutionary for its time. This layout facilitated easier navigation and improved the flow of traffic, while also incorporating wide streets and large public squares, which fostered community interaction. The use of uniform building designs, often featuring neoclassical elements, not only provided a sense of coherence to the rebuilt city but also symbolized the resilience and renewal of the Portuguese spirit.

One of the critical advances during this reconstruction was the introduction of anti-seismic construction techniques. Recognizing the need for structural resilience, Pombal implemented innovative architectural features such as the "pombalino" method of construction, which included wooden frames and flexible materials that allowed buildings to absorb seismic shocks. This forward-thinking approach marked a significant evolution in architectural design, influencing practices not just in Portugal but also in other earthquake-prone regions.

Moreover, the reconstruction of Lisbon also served as a catalyst for broader social and economic reforms. Pombal utilized the rebuilding efforts to implement a series of enlightened policies aimed at modernizing the Portuguese economy, promoting trade, and enhancing public welfare. He bolstered the education system, encouraged the development of the arts and sciences, and sought to diminish the power of the church over civic affairs. These reforms were crucial in reshaping Lisbon into a center of liberal thought and progress.

The reconstruction of Lisbon after the 1755 earthquake thus represented more than just a physical rebuilding; it was a transformative period that laid the foundation for modern Portugal. The ingenuity displayed in urban planning and engineering, coupled with sweeping social reforms, not only revitalized a devastated city but also marked a shift towards a more enlightened and progressive society. Lisbon emerged from the ashes not just as a rebuilt city, but as a symbol of resilience, innovation, and the potential for renewal in the face of calamity—a legacy that continues to resonate in contemporary Portuguese identity.

Economic and Social Reforms

The mid-18th century marked a significant turning point in Portugal's history, primarily due to the ambitions and policies of the Marquis of Pombal, Sebastião José de Carvalho e Melo. Following the catastrophic earthquake of 1755, which devastated Lisbon, Pombal emerged as a central figure in the reconstruction of the city and the broader modernization of the Portuguese economy and society. His reforms were comprehensive, touching upon economic, social, educational, and administrative spheres, and aimed to elevate Portugal's status both domestically and internationally.

Pombal's economic reforms were characterized by a strong emphasis on mercantilism, which sought to enhance state power through the regulation of economic activities. He implemented policies that encouraged agriculture, industry, and trade, aiming to create a self-sufficient economy capable of competing with other European powers. One of his notable initiatives was the promotion of agricultural production. Pombal encouraged the cultivation of new crops, such as potatoes and maize, which were more suited to Portugal's climate and could alleviate food shortages. He also supported the establishment of agricultural schools to educate farmers on modern farming techniques, thereby improving productivity.

In addition to agricultural reform, Pombal recognized the importance of industrial development. He sought to revitalize Portugal's manufacturing sector by creating a favorable environment for artisans and entrepreneurs. The establishment of the Royal Factory of Lace in 1762 and the promotion of silk production exemplified his commitment to fostering local industries. By providing subsidies and tax exemptions, Pombal sought to stimulate domestic manufacturing and reduce reliance on imports.

Trade was another focal point of Pombal's economic strategy. He aimed to expand Portugal's trading networks and sought to enhance the country's position in the Atlantic economy. One of his most significant achievements was the negotiation of treaties that opened new markets for Portuguese goods, particularly in Brazil and Africa. By strengthening trade relations, Pombal hoped to revitalize the Portuguese economy and secure the empire's financial foundations.

Pombal's reforms also extended to social structures, focusing on improving education and public health. He believed that a well-educated populace was essential for the nation's progress. Consequently, he initiated reforms in the educational system, which included the establishment of new schools and the promotion of secular education. Pombal aimed to reduce the influence of the Jesuits in education, which culminated in their expulsion in 1759. This move was not only a political maneuver but also a strategy to promote Enlightenment ideals and modern scientific thought in the education system.

In the realm of public health, Pombal recognized the necessity of addressing the consequences of the 1755 earthquake and subsequent epidemics. He implemented measures to improve urban infrastructure, including the construction of new roads and the renovation of buildings. Pombal's administration also prioritized public health initiatives, such as the establishment of hospitals and health regulations, aiming to create a healthier populace capable of contributing to the nation's productivity.

Moreover, Pombal's social reforms addressed issues of governance and administration. He enacted policies aimed at curbing the power of the nobility and the clergy, redistributing power to the monarchy and the state. This centralization of authority was intended to create a more efficient government that could implement reforms effectively and respond to the needs of the populace.

In conclusion, the economic and social reforms initiated by the Marquis of Pombal laid the groundwork for modernization in Portugal during the 18th century. His multifaceted approach aimed not only at economic revitalization but also at fostering a more educated and healthier society. While his policies faced resistance and criticism, they undeniably contributed to shaping modern Portugal, reinforcing the country's aspirations for progress and enhancing its global standing during a transformative period in European history.

The Expulsion of the Jesuits

The expulsion of the Jesuits from Portugal in 1759 was a pivotal episode in the country's history, reflecting a complex interplay of political, religious, and social factors. This event not only altered the landscape of Portuguese society but also marked a significant moment in the broader context of European Enlightenment and the shifting power dynamics between church and state.

The Jesuit Order, founded in 1540 by St. Ignatius of Loyola, had gained substantial influence throughout Europe and in Portuguese colonies. The society was known for its educational institutions, missionary work, and significant contributions to science and philosophy. However, by the mid-18th century, the Jesuits had become embroiled in political controversies, particularly due to their close ties to the monarchy and their perceived conflicts of interest in both spiritual and temporal affairs.

King José I, influenced by his powerful minister, the Marquis of Pombal, grew increasingly wary of the Jesuits' influence. Pombal, a proponent of Enlightenment ideals, sought to modernize and centralize the Portuguese state, viewing the Jesuits as obstacles to his reform agenda. The Jesuits were often accused of being overly autonomous, wielding considerable economic power through their extensive landholdings and educational institutions, and exerting social influence that sometimes countered the authority of the monarchy.

In 1759, after a series of events that included allegations of conspiracy against the crown, King José I ordered the arrest of Jesuit leaders in Portugal and subsequently expelled the entire order from the kingdom and its territories. This expulsion was not merely a religious act but also a calculated move to diminish the power of the Catholic Church within the state. It signified a profound transformation in the relationship between the monarchy and the church, as the crown sought to assert its control over religious institutions.

The political implications of the Jesuit expulsion extended beyond the immediate context of Portugal. It set a precedent for other European nations grappling with the influence of religious orders in governance. The expulsion resonated with Enlightenment thinkers who advocated for the separation of church and state, and it reflected broader trends of secularization occurring across Europe. The Jesuits' removal from positions of power allowed for the implementation of Pombal's reforms, which aimed to modernize the educational system, promote economic development, and consolidate royal authority.

Religiously, the expulsion had far-reaching consequences for the Catholic Church in Portugal. The loss of the Jesuits, who were among the most educated and influential clergy, weakened the church's capacity to engage in education and missionary work. The void left by the Jesuits was difficult to fill, leading to a decline in the quality of education and the spread of religious teachings in both Portugal and its colonies. Moreover, the event fostered an atmosphere of suspicion toward religious orders, contributing to a growing anti-clerical sentiment that would influence Portuguese society in the ensuing years.

The expulsion also had immediate repercussions in the colonies, particularly in Brazil, where the Jesuits played a crucial role in the education of the indigenous population and the administration of missions. Their removal led to increased tensions and conflicts in these regions, where the vacuum of authority created by their absence often resulted in upheaval and resistance among local populations.

In summary, the expulsion of the Jesuits from Portugal was a significant turning point that reflected the tension between emerging Enlightenment ideals and the established religious order. It underscored the burgeoning power of the state over religious institutions and marked a shift in the socio-political landscape of Portugal, with effects that would resonate well into the modern era. The event not only reshaped the religious fabric of the nation but also laid the groundwork for a new political order that sought to prioritize state interests over ecclesiastical authority.

The Legacy of Pombal

The Marquis of Pombal, Sebastião José de Carvalho e Melo, served as the de facto Prime Minister of Portugal from 1750 to 1777, a transformative period marked by significant political, social, and economic reforms. His legacy is profound, as the policies he instituted laid the groundwork for modernizing Portugal and reshaping the nation's trajectory in the face of domestic and international challenges.

One of Pombal's most notable achievements was the reconstruction of Lisbon following the catastrophic earthquake of 1755. Rather than merely restoring the city to its former state, Pombal seized the opportunity to implement an urban planning vision that emphasized modernity and resilience. The new Baixa district, characterized by its grid layout, wide avenues, and earthquake-resistant buildings, exemplified Enlightenment ideals and served as a model for urban development. This transformation not only altered the physical landscape of Lisbon but also symbolized a shift in thinking toward rationality and progress.

Pombal's economic policies were equally impactful. He initiated a series of reforms aimed at stimulating trade, industry, and agriculture. The establishment of the Companhia Geral do Comércio de Portugal com o Brasil in 1756 sought to centralize and promote commerce with Brazil, enhancing Portugal's economic foothold in its most lucrative colony. Additionally, Pombal's encouragement of agricultural innovation and the promotion of new crops contributed to the diversification of the Portuguese economy, which had long been reliant on its colonial ventures. These economic reforms laid the foundation for a more robust and modern economic structure, although the long-term effects were often stymied by Portugal's continued reliance on its colonial empire.

Moreover, the Marquis of Pombal's approach to governance included the promotion of Enlightenment ideals, which fostered a culture of reason and empiricism in Portugal. He championed education reform, establishing new schools and promoting scientific inquiry. The creation of the Royal Academy of Sciences in 1779 advanced Portugal's intellectual landscape, contributing to a more educated populace that would eventually play a critical role in the nation's political evolution. Pombal's emphasis on education and knowledge also encouraged a shift away from traditional, dogmatic thinking, fostering an environment ripe for the liberal ideas that would emerge in the 19th century. However, Pombal's legacy is not without controversy. His authoritarian methods, particularly in dealing with dissent, created a culture of repression that stifled opposition and led to the expulsion of the Jesuits from Portugal in 1759. This act was not merely a religious purge; it had significant implications for the social fabric of Portuguese society and the role of the Church in governance. The subsequent alienation of the Church and its followers created a schism that would resonate in Portuguese politics for generations.

The long-term effects of Pombal's policies extended beyond his tenure. His reforms laid the groundwork for the eventual emergence of constitutionalism in Portugal during the early 19th century. The ideas of governance and civic rights that he promoted would influence later political movements, culminating in the constitutional revolution of 1820 and the establishment of the constitutional monarchy. Furthermore, the infrastructural and educational advancements initiated under his administration contributed to a gradual modernization process that would be essential for Portugal in the 19th and 20th centuries.

Chapter 8

The Napoleonic Wars and Brazil

The French Invasions of Portugal

The early 19th century marked a tumultuous period in European history, characterized by the rise of Napoleon Bonaparte and the ensuing Napoleonic Wars. Portugal, strategically located on the Iberian Peninsula and with long-standing ties to Britain, found itself caught in the crossfire of these conflicts, leading to a series of invasions that would significantly alter its socio-political landscape.

The roots of Portugal's involvement in the Napoleonic Wars can be traced to its alliance with Britain, formalized by the Anglo-Portuguese Treaty of 1373. This alliance was pivotal, particularly as Portugal sought to maintain its independence and resist French expansionism in the region. As Napoleon's ambitions grew, he aimed to enforce the Continental System, a blockade designed to weaken Britain economically by closing European ports to British trade. Portugal, however, remained a critical trade partner for Britain and refused to comply with the Continental System, leading to escalating tensions with France.

In 1807, the situation reached a boiling point. Napoleon dispatched his forces to invade Portugal, utilizing the pretext that the Portuguese royal family was defying his orders. The French army, under General Junot, entered Lisbon without significant resistance on November 1, 1807. The Portuguese government, recognizing the gravity of the situation, chose to flee rather than confront the French military might. The royal family, led by Prince Regent John, decided to relocate to Brazil, which was then a Portuguese colony. This move not only signified a strategic retreat but also a significant shift in the Portuguese monarchy's center of power.

The French occupation proved to be a tumultuous chapter in Portuguese history. Junot's forces faced immediate challenges in administering the region, as they were met with hostility from the local population. The French imposed heavy taxes and sought to control trade, which alienated many Portuguese citizens. The resistance against the occupation began to coalesce into organized efforts, notably the formation of guerrilla warfare tactics, which marked a significant development in the fight against foreign occupation.

The situation escalated further when, in 1808, the British, recognizing the strategic importance of Portugal, intervened militarily to support the Portuguese resistance against the French. Under the command of Sir Arthur Wellesley—later known as the Duke of Wellington—the British forces landed in Portugal and began a series of campaigns to push the French out of the country. The battles of Roliça and Vimeiro marked the beginning of a concerted effort that would culminate in the liberation of Lisbon in 1808.

Despite initial successes, the conflict continued, resulting in the Second Invasion of Portugal in 1809, when the French, under Marshal Masséna, attempted to regain control. This invasion resulted in a protracted campaign of attrition, with both sides suffering significant losses. The British, utilizing their naval superiority and the support of Portuguese troops, engaged in a series of battles culminating in the decisive victory at the Battle of Bussaco in 1810 and the subsequent lines of Torres Vedras, which fortified Portuguese defenses against further French advances.

The French invasions had profound implications for Portugal. The initial loss of the monarchy to Brazil catalyzed a shift in the political landscape, setting the stage for significant changes in governance and society upon the royal family's return in 1821. Moreover, the experience of occupation and resistance fostered a growing sense of national identity and unity among the Portuguese people.

In summary, the French invasions of Portugal were not merely a conflict between two nations but rather a pivotal moment that drew Portugal into the broader European struggle against Napoleonic hegemony. The ramifications of these invasions extended far beyond the battlefield, influencing Portugal's political evolution and its place in the world in the years that followed.

The Flight of the Portuguese Court to Brazil

In the early 19th century, Portugal found itself engulfed in the turmoil of the Napoleonic Wars. The invasion of Portugal by French troops in 1807 marked a pivotal moment in the nation's history, leading to the extraordinary decision by the Portuguese royal family to relocate to Brazil. This relocation not only altered the course of the Portuguese monarchy but also reshaped the political, social, and economic landscape of both Portugal and its largest colony.

The decision to flee was prompted by the advancing French army, which threatened to take control of Portugal. The Prince Regent, João VI, and his court realized that remaining in Portugal could lead to their capture and the subsequent imposition of French influence over the Portuguese crown. In November 1807, under the cover of night, the royal family and approximately 15,000 people—including nobles, government officials, and soldiers—embarked on a perilous journey across the Atlantic Ocean. The fleet, which included multiple ships laden with essential documents, treasures, and artworks, arrived in Brazil in early 1808.

The relocation to Brazil had immediate and profound effects on the colony. Once considered merely an outpost of the Portuguese Empire, Brazil was transformed into the center of Portuguese governance. The royal family's presence legitimized Brazil's status and brought an influx of resources and attention. João VI established a court in Rio de Janeiro, which became the de facto capital of the Portuguese Empire. This not only elevated the political significance of Brazil but also attracted European intellectuals, artists, and merchants, leading to a cultural flourishing that blended Portuguese and indigenous influences.

The royal court's arrival had significant economic implications as well. The Portuguese government implemented reforms that modernized Brazilian infrastructure and economy, including the establishment of a banking system, the promotion of agriculture, and the expansion of trade. The port of Rio de Janeiro was opened to foreign trade, allowing for increased commerce and the introduction of new goods and ideas. These changes contributed to Brazil's economic growth, fundamentally altering its relationship with Portugal and the greater world.

However, the presence of the royal family in Brazil also led to tensions between the two regions. The Portuguese elites in Brazil began to assert their interests, often at odds with those of the monarchy in Lisbon. This growing sense of autonomy among Brazilian elites was crucial in the subsequent push for independence. The Brazilian population, inspired by the Enlightenment ideals of liberty and self-determination, increasingly viewed the royal family as out of touch with local needs and aspirations. When João VI returned to Portugal in

1821, leaving his son, Dom Pedro, in charge as regent, the stage was set for a burgeoning independence movement.

Dom Pedro's decision to declare Brazil's independence from Portugal in 1822 was a direct consequence of this historical flight. The royal family's relocation had inadvertently sown the seeds of nationalism and self-governance in Brazil. The subsequent conflict would lead to the establishment of Brazil as an independent empire, further complicating Portugal's colonial ambitions and shifting the balance of power within the empire itself.

In conclusion, the flight of the Portuguese court to Brazil during the Napoleonic Wars was a transformative event that not only reshaped the dynamics of the Portuguese Empire but also laid the groundwork for Brazil's emergence as an independent nation. This pivotal moment illustrated the interconnectedness of political decisions and their far-reaching implications, highlighting how a royal family's relocation could catalyze monumental shifts in colonial governance, economic practices, and national identity. The legacy of this event continues to influence the historical narratives of both Portugal and Brazil, underscoring the complexities of empire and independence.

The Peninsular War

The Peninsular War (1808-1814) was a significant military conflict that emerged as a part of the broader Napoleonic Wars. It encompassed the struggle for control of the Iberian Peninsula, primarily focusing on Spain and Portugal. Portugal's involvement in this war was marked by its unique geopolitical position, alliance with Britain, and the profound impact it had on the nation's socio-political landscape.

Background to the Conflict

The war's roots can be traced back to the aggressive expansionist policies of Napoleon Bonaparte, who sought to dominate Europe. In 1807, under the guise of enforcing the Continental System against Britain, French troops invaded Portugal. The Portuguese royal family, then led by Prince Regent João VI, fled to Brazil to escape the advancing French army. This evacuation not only symbolized the immediate threat posed by Napoleon but also set a precedent for the emergence of Brazil as a focal point of Portuguese governance during the conflict.

The Invasion and British Alliance

Upon invading Portugal, Napoleon sought to install a puppet government that would align with French interests. However, the Portuguese people did not passively accept foreign rule. The British, recognizing the strategic importance of Portugal, quickly intervened. Under the command of General Sir Arthur Wellesley, later known as the Duke of Wellington, British forces landed in Portugal to support Portuguese resistance against the French.

The first significant military engagement occurred in 1808 at the Battle of Vimeiro, where British and Portuguese troops successfully repelled a French assault. The subsequent Convention of Sintra allowed for a temporary cessation of hostilities, but tensions remained high. The French, undeterred, regrouped and returned to the offensive.

The Guerrilla Warfare

One of the defining characteristics of the conflict in Portugal was the rise of guerrilla warfare. Portuguese partisans, often referred to as "guerrilleros," played a crucial role in undermining French operations. Utilizing their intimate knowledge of the terrain, these fighters engaged in hit-and-run tactics, disrupting supply lines and communication for the French forces. Their efforts not only weakened the enemy but also galvanized nationalistic sentiments among the Portuguese populace, fostering a spirit of resistance that would ultimately contribute to the liberation of the country.

The Campaigns and Key Battles

The Peninsular War saw several critical campaigns and battles within Portugal. The Second Battle of Porto in 1809 marked a significant victory for the Anglo-Portuguese forces, leading to the retreat of French troops from the north of Portugal. The defensive strategies employed by Wellington, including the use of the Lines of Torres Vedras, effectively fortified Lisbon against a potential French siege. This series of entrenched positions around Lisbon exemplified military innovation and strategic foresight, ultimately thwarting Napoleon's ambitions in the region.

The Liberation and Aftermath

As the war progressed, the tide turned against the French. By 1811, the combined forces of the British, Portuguese, and Spanish were systematically pushing the French out of the Iberian Peninsula. The culmination of these efforts came in 1814 when the last of the French troops were expelled from Portugal. The war had a lasting impact on the nation, leading to increased national consciousness and a sense of unity among the Portuguese people.

The aftermath of the Peninsular War left Portugal with a mixed legacy. While the country regained its sovereignty, the conflict had drained its resources and destabilized its economy. The royal family's return from Brazil marked the beginning of significant political changes, ultimately leading to the Portuguese Liberal Wars and shaping the future trajectory of the nation.

In conclusion, Portugal's role in the Peninsular War was pivotal not only in the context of military engagements but also in the broader narrative of national identity and resistance against foreign domination. The conflict catalyzed significant transformations within Portugal, influencing its political landscape and contributing to the eventual emergence of a modern nation-state.

The Return of the Court and the Independence of Brazil

The early 19th century was a tumultuous period for both Portugal and its largest colony, Brazil. The Napoleonic Wars had forced the Portuguese royal family to take unprecedented measures to ensure their survival and the integrity of their realm. In 1807, with the threat of French invasion looming, King João VI made a momentous decision: he and the Portuguese court would flee to Brazil. This relocation marked a significant turning point in the relationship between Portugal and its colony, setting the stage for Brazil's eventual independence.

Upon their arrival in Rio de Janeiro, the Portuguese royal family quickly established the city as the de facto capital of the Portuguese Empire. The court's presence in Brazil brought substantial changes to the colony. The influx of nobility and officials resulted in the rapid urbanization of Rio, transforming it into a vibrant political and cultural center. The Portuguese court introduced a range of reforms aimed at modernizing colonial governance and infrastructure. They established institutions such as banks, schools, and cultural organizations, effectively elevating Brazil's status within the empire.

However, this newfound prominence also sowed the seeds of discontent. Many Brazilians began to resent the concentration of power in the hands of the Portuguese elite and the continued economic exploitation of the colony. While the court flourished, the local population faced high taxes and restrictions on trade that benefitted only the Portuguese interests. Additionally, the arrival of the court led to a rise in nationalism among Brazilian elites, who started to envision a future where Brazil could be independent and self-governing.

As the Napoleonic Wars began to wane and the threat of invasion diminished, King João VI faced increasing pressure to return to Portugal. In 1820, a liberal revolution erupted in Portugal, demanding constitutional reforms and the restoration of the monarchy's authority. The revolution prompted King João VI to consider returning to Portugal, but his decision was fraught with complications. The revolutionary government in Portugal sought to reassert control over Brazil, which alarmed many Brazilian leaders who had grown accustomed to autonomy under royal rule.

The tensions escalated further when João VI returned to Portugal in 1821, leaving his son, Dom Pedro, as regent in Brazil. Dom Pedro became a focal point for growing sentiments of independence among Brazilians. The situation reached a boiling point in 1822 when the Portuguese Cortes (parliament) attempted to impose restrictions on Brazil's autonomy, including the demand that Dom Pedro return to Portugal.

In response, Dom Pedro took a decisive stand. On September 7, 1822, he declared Brazil's independence from Portugal in a dramatic proclamation known as the "Grito do Ipiranga" ("Cry of Ipiranga"). This moment marked the birth of the independent Brazilian nation, with Dom Pedro becoming its first emperor, Dom Pedro I. His declaration was fueled by a combination of nationalist fervor, a desire for self-governance, and the rejection of Portuguese attempts to reinstate colonial control.

The aftermath of Brazil's independence was complex. While the transition was relatively peaceful compared to many independence movements in Latin America, it resulted in significant political and social upheaval. Brazil's independence was recognized by Portugal in 1825, following a treaty that required Brazil to pay a hefty indemnity to the Portuguese crown, reflecting the complexities of their intertwined histories.

In summary, the return of the Portuguese court to Brazil catalyzed a series of events that ultimately led to Brazil's independence in 1822. The experience of royal governance in Brazil fostered a burgeoning sense of national identity and autonomy that would shape the course of Brazilian history for decades to come.

The Impact of Brazil's Independence on Portugal

The independence of Brazil in 1822 marked a significant turning point in Portugal's history, reverberating across its economy, political landscape, and global standing. Brazil had been the crown jewel of the Portuguese Empire, contributing immensely to its wealth and influence. The loss of this vast territory would therefore have profound implications that would shape Portugal's trajectory in the 19th century and beyond.

Economic Consequences

Brazil's independence resulted in an immediate and severe economic impact on Portugal. Prior to independence, Brazil was the primary source of lucrative exports such as sugar, coffee, and gold. The colonial economy was deeply intertwined with that of the mother country, with a significant portion of Portugal's budget derived from revenues generated in Brazil. The sudden loss of this revenue stream led to a fiscal crisis in Portugal. The government faced a steep decline in income, leading to increased national debt and economic instability.

In the aftermath of independence, Portugal struggled to adjust to the new economic reality. The sharp decline in trade with Brazil imploded the mercantile structures that had been in place for centuries. Previously, Portuguese merchants had dominated the Brazilian market; now, Brazil sought to establish its own commercial relationships with other nations, thereby diminishing Portugal's economic influence. The loss of Brazil forced Portugal to rethink its economic policies and attempt to strengthen trade relationships with other colonies, particularly in Africa and Asia, but many of these territories were not as economically viable as Brazil.

Political Ramifications

Politically, the loss of Brazil exposed the vulnerabilities of the Portuguese monarchy. The royal family had relocated to Brazil during the Napoleonic Wars, and their return after independence was fraught with challenges. The political landscape in Portugal became tumultuous as factions emerged, advocating for various forms of governance, from absolutism to liberal constitutionalism. The monarchy's weakened stature led to political instability, which was compounded by social unrest and economic hardship.

The discontent among the populace eventually contributed to a series of revolutions and civil wars, notably the Liberal Wars in the 1820s and 1830s, as various groups vied for power in a rapidly changing political environment. This internal conflict diverted attention from colonial affairs and weakened Portugal's ability to maintain its remaining overseas territories.

Global Standing and International Relations

Brazil's independence also had significant implications for Portugal's standing on the global stage. Once a formidable maritime empire, Portugal found itself diminished and struggling to assert its influence. The loss of Brazil not only reduced its territorial holdings but also altered the perception of Portugal as a colonial power. Other nations, observing Portugal's weakened position, began to challenge its remaining colonies, leading to further territorial losses in Africa and Asia.

Moreover, Brazil's independence inspired other colonies and territories under Portuguese rule, particularly in Africa, to pursue their own aspirations for independence. This wave of decolonization during the 19th and 20th centuries would lead to the eventual dismantling of the Portuguese Empire, further emphasizing the long-term implications of Brazil's secession.

Chapter 9

The Liberal Wars and Constitutionalism

The Constitutional Revolution of 1820

The Constitutional Revolution of 1820 marked a pivotal moment in Portuguese history, symbolizing the struggle between traditional monarchy and emerging liberal ideals. The roots of this revolution can be traced back to the broader European Enlightenment, which emphasized reason, individual rights, and the need for government accountability. These liberal ideas began to permeate Portuguese society in the late 18th and early 19th centuries, fueled by discontent with absolutist rule and the socio-political turmoil experienced during the Napoleonic Wars.

The backdrop to the revolution was characterized by political instability and economic hardship. The French invasions of Portugal and the subsequent relocation of the Portuguese royal family to Brazil highlighted the vulnerabilities of the monarchy. This period saw the rise of a burgeoning middle class that increasingly sought political representation and reform. The lack of effective governance, coupled with a growing sense of nationalism, created fertile ground for revolutionary sentiment.

In 1820, a military-led uprising in Porto catalyzed the revolution. The insurrection was sparked by a combination of grievances against the monarchy, including economic distress, social inequality, and a desire for greater political freedoms. The revolutionaries sought to establish a constitutional government that would limit the powers of the king and protect the rights of citizens. The call for a constitutional monarchy resonated deeply, as it promised to align Portugal with the liberal movements sweeping across Europe.

The revolution quickly gained momentum, and by August 1820, the revolutionary forces had successfully gained control of Lisbon, compelling King João VI to accept the establishment of a constitutional government. The Constitution of 1822 was subsequently drafted, inspired by the liberal principles of the French Revolution and the constitutional framework of other European nations. It included provisions for civil liberties, freedom of the press, and the establishment of a parliamentary system. This was a significant shift from the absolutist rule that had defined Portugal for centuries.

However, the revolutionary fervor was met with considerable resistance. The conservative factions, including royalists and the Catholic Church, opposed the constitutional changes, fearing that they would undermine traditional authority and social order. The tension between liberal and conservative forces led to a period of instability, culminating in the dissolution of the 1822 Constitution just a few months after its enactment. The monarchy attempted to reassert its authority, leading to a civil war known as the Liberal Wars (1828-1834), which further deepened the ideological divides within Portuguese society.

Despite the initial setbacks, the Constitutional Revolution of 1820 laid the groundwork for a more enduring shift towards liberal governance in Portugal. It marked the beginning of a protracted struggle for political reform, ultimately resulting in the establishment of a constitutional monarchy that persisted into the late 19th century. The ideas and aspirations that emerged during this revolution continued to influence future generations, shaping the trajectory of Portuguese political development.

In summary, the Constitutional Revolution of 1820 was a critical juncture in Portugal's history, driven by the interplay of liberal ideas and the desire for reform. While it faced immediate challenges, the revolution set in motion a transformative process that would redefine the relationship between the state and its citizens, fostering an environment that embraced democratic ideals and civil liberties. This period not only reflected the aspirations of the Portuguese people but also mirrored the broader European trends towards liberalism and constitutional governance, leaving an indelible mark on the nation's political landscape.

The Miguelite Wars

The Miguelite Wars, fought between the years 1828 and 1834, represent a significant chapter in Portuguese history, characterized by the struggle for political power between liberal forces advocating for constitutional governance and absolutist factions seeking to restore monarchical authority under Miguel I. This civil war was not merely a clash of arms but a profound confrontation of ideologies that shaped the future of Portugal and its governance.

The backdrop to the Miguelite Wars can be traced to the constitutional revolution of 1820, which led to the establishment of a constitutional monarchy in Portugal. Following the revolution, King João VI returned from Brazil, where he had fled during the Napoleonic Wars, and was compelled to accept a constitutional charter. However, the death of João VI in 1826 precipitated a succession crisis. His son, Pedro IV, briefly ascended to the throne but, in an act of political pragmatism, abdicated in favor of his daughter, Maria II, who was only a child at the time.

Pedro IV's abdication was contentious, as it opened the door for Miguel, the king's younger brother, who had been raised in an absolutist tradition and opposed the constitutional changes. In 1828, Miguel seized the throne, declaring himself king and effectively nullifying the constitutional monarchy. This act ignited a civil war, as liberal factions rallied to support the rightful claim of Maria II, leading to the division of the country between liberal and absolutist forces.

The Miguelite Wars can be characterized by a series of battles and political maneuvers, as both sides sought to consolidate their power. The liberals, bolstered by the support of various social groups including the military, the bourgeoisie, and segments of the peasantry, organized themselves under the banner of the Constitutionalists. Meanwhile, Miguel's forces attracted support from conservative elements within the clergy and the aristocracy, who feared the liberal reforms that threatened their traditional privileges.

The conflict saw several notable battles, including the Battle of Santarém in 1831, which marked a significant victory for the liberal forces. However, the war was not just a series of military engagements; it was also deeply entrenched in the national psyche and social fabric of Portugal. The war was marked by brutal reprisals, as both sides committed atrocities against each other's supporters. The division was not merely political; it manifested in communities, families, and social networks, creating a legacy of mistrust that would endure long after the conflict had ended.

Internationally, the Miguelite Wars drew attention, particularly from the British, who favored liberalism and were concerned about the potential for a resurgence of absolutist regimes in Europe. The involvement of foreign powers, particularly the British who supported the liberal cause, played a critical role in altering the balance of power. The eventual liberal victory was secured in 1834, following the intervention of foreign allies and the exhaustion of Miguel's forces.

The war concluded with the defeat of Miguel, who fled to exile, while Maria II was restored to the throne. The Miguelite Wars had far-reaching consequences, leading to the consolidation of liberal constitutionalism in Portugal and the establishment of a more modern state. However, the conflict also left deep scars, fostering animosities that would influence Portuguese politics for decades.

In summary, the Miguelite Wars were not merely a battle for the throne; they were emblematic of a broader struggle between tradition and modernity, absolutism and constitutional democracy. This civil war laid the groundwork for the future of Portugal's political landscape, demonstrating the complexities of governance in a society grappling with rapid change and the demands of competing ideologies. The legacy of the Miguelite Wars continues to resonate in contemporary discussions about democracy and governance in Portugal.

The Role of British Influence in the Liberal Wars

The Liberal Wars in Portugal, also known as the Miguelite Wars, were a series of civil conflicts that occurred between 1828 and 1834, primarily revolving around the struggle between liberal constitutionalists and absolutist monarchists. The outcome of these wars was significantly shaped by British influence, which played a crucial role in the political dynamics of the period.

At the center of the conflict was the rivalry between the supporters of the deposed King Pedro IV, who championed a constitutional monarchy, and his brother, Miguel, who sought to restore absolute monarchy. The Portuguese constitutionalists, who had gained traction during the Liberal Revolution of 1820, faced immense challenges from Miguel's forces, which were determined to reestablish traditional monarchical authority. The stakes were not just national; the conflicts were emblematic of broader European struggles between liberalism and conservatism.

Britain's involvement in the Liberal Wars was motivated by a combination of strategic interests and ideological sympathies. The British government, under the influence of liberal thinkers and policymakers, sought to promote constitutional governance and stability throughout Europe, particularly in the context of rising nationalist movements and the decline of absolute monarchies.

Britain was also keen on securing favorable trade relations with Portugal, given its historical ties and economic interests, especially in the context of the lucrative wine trade.

British support for the liberal cause manifested in several ways. First and foremost, it provided military assistance. The British government allowed the Portuguese constitutionalists to recruit and train volunteer forces in Britain, which included experienced soldiers who had previously served in various European conflicts. This influx of trained personnel bolstered the ranks of the liberal forces, enabling them to better confront Miguel's royalist troops.

Moreover, Britain's naval power played a critical role in the conflict. The British Navy maintained a presence in the Mediterranean and off the coast of Portugal, which served as a deterrent against foreign intervention, particularly from Spain, which had been sympathetic to Miguel's cause. The British blockade of Miguel's supply lines hampered his ability to sustain his forces, effectively tipping the balance in favor of the liberals.

In addition to military support, British diplomatic efforts were instrumental in garnering international recognition for the constitutionalist cause. British diplomats engaged in negotiations with other European powers, advocating for the legitimacy of the constitutionalists and isolating Miguel's regime. This diplomatic maneuvering helped to solidify support for the liberal factions while undermining the absolutist claims of Miguel.

The ideological underpinnings of British support were also significant. British intellectuals and political leaders viewed the Liberal Wars as part of a larger struggle for democratic governance and individual rights across Europe. This sense of shared purpose galvanized public opinion in Britain, resulting in popular support for the Portuguese liberals. The British press played an influential role in shaping narratives that favored the constitutionalists, portraying them as champions of progress against the forces of tyranny.

Ultimately, the Liberal Wars concluded in 1834 with the defeat of Miguel's forces and the establishment of a constitutional monarchy under King Pedro IV. The British influence during this tumultuous period was pivotal; it not only provided essential military and diplomatic support but also reinforced the ideological framework that underpinned the liberal movement. The outcome of the wars marked a significant turning point in Portuguese history, ushering in an era characterized by constitutional governance and the gradual modernization of the state, reflecting the enduring impact of British engagement in Portugal's struggle for liberalism.

In summary, British support was crucial in shaping the outcome of the Liberal Wars, as it provided the necessary military, diplomatic, and ideological backing that allowed the constitutionalists to emerge victorious, thereby altering the trajectory of Portuguese governance and society for decades to come.

The Establishment of Constitutional Monarchy in Portugal

The early 19th century in Portugal was marked by a profound political transformation, culminating in the establishment of a constitutional monarchy. This shift was rooted in a complex interplay of Enlightenment ideas, social unrest, and the influence of broader European political movements. The backdrop to this evolution includes the backdrop of the Constitutional Revolution of 1820, which emerged from the struggle against absolutism and the desire for a more representative government.

The Revolution of 1820 was instigated by a coalition of liberal intellectuals and military officers who were inspired by the principles of the French Revolution and the liberal movements sweeping across Europe. This burgeoning liberal sentiment contrasted sharply with the absolutist rule of King John VI, who had fled to Brazil during the Napoleonic Wars. The return of the monarchy to Portugal in 1821 was met with significant pressure from the revolutionaries, who demanded a constitutional framework that would limit royal powers and establish a parliamentary system.

In response to the revolutionary fervor, the Cortes (the Portuguese parliament) convened and drafted the Constitution of 1822. This document was a landmark in Portuguese history, emphasizing popular sovereignty, individual rights, and the separation of powers. The Constitution established a constitutional monarchy, where the king retained executive authority but was bound by the laws enacted by the Cortes. This marked a significant departure from the absolute monarchy that had characterized the country for centuries.

However, the implementation of the constitutional monarchy was fraught with challenges. The Constitution of 1822 was short-lived, as political tensions between liberal and conservative factions led to its suspension just a year later. The ensuing period was characterized by a power struggle that manifested in the Miguelite Wars (1828-1834), where absolutist forces loyal to King Miguel sought to dismantle the constitutional framework established by the liberals. The civil war ultimately resulted in the victory of the constitutionalists and the restoration of the constitutional monarchy under Queen Maria II.

The new constitutional order, established in 1834, stabilized the political landscape and facilitated the gradual development of a parliamentary system. The Charter of 1834, which replaced the earlier constitution, provided a more moderate framework that aimed to balance the interests of various political factions while ensuring civil liberties and the role of the monarchy. It instituted a bicameral legislature, consisting of the Chamber of Deputies and the House of Peers, thus formalizing the legislative process and providing a platform for political debate.

Throughout the 19th century, the constitutional monarchy underwent several modifications, as competing political factions vied for power. The Liberal Party and the Conservative Party emerged as the dominant political forces, each advocating for differing visions of governance. The political instability during this period was characterized by frequent changes in government, with cabinet ministries shifting in response to popular pressure and electoral outcomes. Despite these challenges, the constitutional monarchy played a crucial role in modernizing Portugal, paving the way for social and economic reforms.

The establishment of the constitutional monarchy also had implications for the role of the Catholic Church, which had traditionally been a powerful institution in Portuguese society. The liberal government sought to curtail the Church's influence in political matters, leading to tensions between church and state that reverberated throughout the century.

In conclusion, the establishment of a constitutional monarchy in Portugal represented a pivotal moment in the nation's history. It marked the transition from absolutism to a more representative form of governance, deeply influencing the political landscape of Portugal. While the path was fraught with conflict and instability, the constitutional framework laid the foundations for modern democracy in Portugal, contributing to the evolution of political institutions and the rights of citizens that continue to resonate in contemporary Portuguese society.

The Decline of Monarchical Power

The decline of monarchical power in Portugal, particularly in the 19th century, marked a significant transition in the nation's governance and political landscape. This period was characterized by growing liberal sentiments, widespread calls for reform, and the emergence of political movements that sought to challenge the traditional authority of the monarchy. The culmination of these forces led to the gradual erosion of monarchical influence and the establishment of a constitutional framework that would redefine Portugal's political identity.

The early 19th century was a time of profound upheaval in Europe, influenced by the Enlightenment ideals that championed reason, individual rights, and democratic governance. In Portugal, these ideas found fertile ground among a populace weary of the autocratic tendencies of the monarchy, particularly under the rule of King Miguel I, who reigned from 1828 to 1834. Miguel's authoritarian regime, marked by repression and a refusal to recognize the constitutional liberties established earlier in the Liberal Revolution of 1820, incited widespread discontent among liberal factions.

The Liberal Wars, also known as the Miguelite Wars (1828-1834), emerged as a direct response to Miguel's absolutism. These conflicts were not merely civil wars; they represented a broader struggle between the forces of liberalism and conservatism. The liberal factions, primarily composed of middle-class professionals, landowners, and intellectuals, sought to restore constitutional governance and dismantle the entrenched privileges of the monarchy and the nobility. Their efforts were bolstered by support from Britain, which endorsed liberal reforms throughout Europe and provided critical military assistance to the liberal cause in Portugal.

The eventual victory of the liberal forces in 1834 marked a pivotal moment in Portuguese history. With the defeat of Miguel's forces, the constitutional monarchy was reinstated, albeit in a weakened state. The new constitutional framework limited the powers of the monarchy, establishing a parliamentary system where elected representatives held significant authority. This shift not only curtailed the monarch's ability to govern unilaterally but also laid the groundwork for a political culture that favored democratic engagement and accountability.

As the 19th century progressed, the monarchy's influence continued to wane. Political instability, characterized by frequent changes in government and the rise of political factions, further undermined royal authority. The burgeoning political parties, including the progressive and reactionary factions, began to dominate the political landscape, challenging the monarchy's role in governance. The monarchy, which once symbolized stability and continuity, increasingly came to be seen as an obstacle to progress and reform.

Additionally, social changes, driven by urbanization and the rise of a commercial economy, contributed to the declining influence of the monarchy. A growing middle class, empowered by economic opportunities and influenced by liberal ideas, began to assert its voice in political matters. This new social order demanded representation and rights, further eroding the traditional bases of monarchical power.

The culmination of these factors led to a shift in public sentiment. The monarchy struggled to maintain relevance in a rapidly changing society that increasingly valued democratic principles and individual rights over hereditary privilege. The assassination of King Carlos I in 1908 and the subsequent political turmoil signaled the monarchy's vulnerability, ultimately culminating in the Republican Revolution of 1910, which abolished the monarchy and established the First Portuguese Republic.

In conclusion, the decline of monarchical power in Portugal was a complex interplay of liberal ideals, political conflict, social change, and the emergence of a more active and demanding citizenry. The monarchy's inability to adapt to the evolving political landscape and its failure to reconcile with the burgeoning demands for democracy marked the end of an era and the beginning of a new political reality for the Portuguese people. The legacy of this decline continues to resonate in modern Portugal, as the nation grapples with the historical implications of its monarchical past within a contemporary democratic framework.

Chapter 10

The First Republic

The Revolution of 1910

The Revolution of 1910 marked a pivotal moment in Portuguese history, signifying the transition from a constitutional monarchy to a republic. This transformation was not only a political shift but also a reflection of broader social, economic, and ideological changes that had been brewing in Portugal for decades.

For much of the 19th century, Portugal was plagued by political instability, characterized by a series of short-lived governments and frequent changes in leadership. The monarchy, represented by King Carlos I, faced mounting criticism and dissatisfaction from various sectors of society, including the burgeoning middle class, intellectuals, and republican activists. The socio-economic backdrop was marked by widespread poverty and inequality, particularly in rural areas, while urban centers grappled with industrialization and modernization that often left traditional structures in disarray.

The monarchy's inability to address these pressing issues led to growing discontent. The assassination of King Carlos I and his heir, Prince Luís Filipe, in 1908 by a group of republican militants highlighted the fragility of the royal authority and catalyzed revolutionary sentiments. The political turmoil that ensued further weakened the monarchy's grip on power, and the disillusionment with the existing regime intensified.

By 1910, the Portuguese Republican Party had gained significant traction, advocating for a radical overhaul of the political system. Their calls for a republic resonated with a populace increasingly frustrated with the monarchy's failure to implement necessary reforms. The republicans, alongside various social movements and labor organizations, began organizing strikes and protests, effectively challenging the status quo.

On the night of October 3, 1910, the revolution was set in motion by the Republicans, who launched a coordinated uprising. The insurrection began in

Lisbon, where republican forces gathered to seize key locations, including government buildings and military barracks. The revolutionaries faced initial resistance from royalist troops, but the tide turned as the military began to defect to the republican cause. In a matter of days, the revolution gained momentum, culminating in the flight of King Manuel II, the last reigning monarch of Portugal, to exile.

As the monarchy crumbled, the republicans declared the establishment of the Portuguese Republic on October 5, 1910. The new government, formed under the leadership of prominent republican figures such as Afonso Costa and Manuel de Arriaga, sought to implement sweeping reforms aimed at modernizing the nation and addressing the socio-economic grievances that had fueled the revolution. The republicans envisioned a secular and democratic state, emphasizing civil liberties, education, and social justice.

However, the path to a stable republic was fraught with challenges. The early years of the Portuguese Republic were marked by political fragmentation, with numerous parties vying for power and frequent changes in government. The republic faced significant opposition from monarchists and conservative factions that were unwilling to accept the new order. Additionally, social unrest and labor strikes persisted as the new government struggled to address the pressing economic issues facing the nation.

Despite these challenges, the Revolution of 1910 fundamentally altered the trajectory of Portuguese history. It represented a decisive break from the past, embodying the aspirations of a society seeking greater political representation and social equity. The establishment of the republic fostered a new sense of national identity and laid the groundwork for subsequent political developments, including the tumultuous years leading to the Estado Novo regime and the eventual democratization of Portugal in the late 20th century.

In conclusion, the Revolution of 1910 was a defining moment in Portugal's history, marking the end of monarchical rule and paving the way for a republican government. While the transition was met with significant challenges, it reflected the growing desire for a more inclusive and equitable political system, ultimately shaping the future of the nation.

Political Instability and Social Change in Early 20th Century Portugal

The establishment of the Portuguese First Republic in 1910 marked a significant turning point in the nation's history, representing the culmination of a long struggle against monarchical rule. However, this transition was fraught with political instability and social challenges that would shape the trajectory of the republic in its formative years. The period following the revolution was characterized by a series of governmental upheavals, social unrest, and economic difficulties that tested the resilience of the newly established regime.

In the wake of the revolution, the First Republic faced immediate challenges. The political landscape was fragmented, with a plethora of political parties vying for power, often leading to short-lived governments. The initial euphoria of republicanism quickly gave way to political disillusionment as the new government struggled to assert authority and legitimacy. Between 1910 and 1926, Portugal saw over 40 different governments, indicative of the chronic instability that plagued the republic. This incessant turnover of leadership not only hampered effective governance but also fostered an environment of political cynicism among the populace.

The fragmentation of political parties was exacerbated by ideological divisions. The republic encompassed a range of political ideologies, from radical leftists seeking sweeping social reforms to moderate liberal factions advocating for stability and gradual change. This ideological spectrum led to intense rivalries and conflicts, further complicating the political landscape. The inability of political leaders to form cohesive coalitions resulted in a lack of effective policy implementation, which alienated many citizens who had hoped for meaningful reforms following the monarchy's fall.

Social change during this period was equally tumultuous. The First Republic aimed to modernize Portuguese society through various reforms, including the secularization of education and the promotion of civil liberties. However, these reforms often met with resistance from conservative factions, particularly the Catholic Church, which had played a significant role in Portuguese life under the monarchy. The Church's opposition was rooted in a desire to maintain its influence over social and political matters, leading to a cultural clash that further destabilized the republic.

Economic challenges compounded the difficulties faced by the First Republic. The country was grappling with the aftermath of the 1918 influenza pandemic, which had devastating effects on the population and economy. Additionally, Portugal's involvement in World War I, albeit limited, strained resources and diverted attention from pressing domestic issues. The war exacerbated economic instability, leading to inflation and rising unemployment, which fueled social discontent. Strikes and protests became common as workers demanded better wages and conditions, reflecting the growing rift between the government and the working class.

The political instability and economic turmoil ultimately created fertile ground for radical movements. The military, discontent with the government's inability to address the chaos, began to play an increasingly influential role in politics. By the mid-1920s, the military's frustration culminated in a coup d'état, leading to the end of the First Republic and the establishment of a military dictatorship.

In summary, the early years of the First Republic in Portugal were marked by significant political instability and social upheaval. The challenges of fragmented governance, ideological divisions, economic hardship, and resistance from traditional institutions created a volatile environment that ultimately undermined the republic's goals. These factors not only shaped the trajectory of Portugal in the 20th century but also laid the groundwork for the authoritarian regimes that would follow. The lessons from this period highlight the complexities of democratic transitions and the vital importance of stability and consensus in achieving lasting political change.

Portugal in World War I

Portugal's involvement in World War I, while often overshadowed by the actions of larger European powers, was significant both in terms of military engagement and the impact on the nation's future. Initially, Portugal maintained a position of neutrality at the outbreak of the war in 1914, a stance that was in line with its historical policy of non-intervention in European conflicts. However, several factors ultimately led to its entry into the war in 1916.

One of the primary motivators for Portugal's involvement was its longstanding alliance with Britain, formalized through the Anglo-Portuguese Treaty of 1373. As the war unfolded, Britain sought support from its allies to bolster its military resources, especially in the context of securing its colonies and trade routes.

Portugal's colonies in Africa, particularly Angola and Mozambique, were considered vital for safeguarding British interests against German expansion. Additionally, the Portuguese government was motivated by a desire to reclaim its international standing, which had been diminished in the years leading up to the war.

In March 1916, after a series of provocations from Germany, including the sinking of Portuguese ships, Portugal formally declared war on Germany. This marked a pivotal moment as it aligned the nation with the Allies, joining the fight against the Central Powers. The Portuguese military mobilized quickly, and the government began to organize a significant expeditionary force, known as the Portuguese Expeditionary Corps (CEP), to be deployed to the Western Front.

The CEP was deployed to France in 1917, where it participated in several key battles, most notably the Battle of La Lys in April 1918. This engagement aimed to support the Allied forces against a German offensive. Unfortunately, the Portuguese troops faced severe challenges, including inadequate training, poor equipment, and logistical difficulties. The Battle of La Lys resulted in heavy casualties for the Portuguese forces, with thousands of soldiers killed or wounded, which led to a demoralizing impact on the national psyche.

Domestically, the war catalyzed significant social and political changes in Portugal. The hardships brought about by the conflict, coupled with economic strain and military failures, fueled widespread dissatisfaction with the ruling monarchy. Public sentiment began to shift towards republicanism, culminating in political unrest and social upheaval. By 1917, Portugal was experiencing strikes and protests, which reflected the mounting frustrations of a populace weary of the war's toll.

The end of World War I in 1918 did not bring peace for Portugal. Instead, the aftermath of the war revealed the deep fractures within Portuguese society. The Treaty of Versailles, which concluded the conflict, altered the geopolitical landscape of Europe and left Portugal grappling with the consequences of its military involvement. The loss of life and resources strained the economy, and the perceived failures on the battlefield further weakened support for the monarchy. This culminated in the Revolution of 1910, which transitioned Portugal from a monarchy to a republic.

In summary, Portugal's role in World War I was marked by a complex interplay of international alliances, national aspirations, and social upheaval. The war not only shaped Portugal's immediate military and political landscape but also set the stage for profound changes in the years that followed. The legacy of the Great War would continue to influence Portugal's trajectory, as the nation sought to redefine itself in the wake of conflict and the transition to republicanism.

Economic Turmoil and Financial Crisis in the First Republic

The First Republic of Portugal, established in 1910 following the revolution that deposed the monarchy, was marked by a tumultuous economic landscape that significantly impacted the nation's trajectory. The immediate aftermath of the revolution brought about a profound transformation in governance and societal structure, yet it was accompanied by persistent economic challenges that would ultimately contribute to the republic's instability and decline.

Initially, the republic faced the daunting task of reconstructing a nation that had been steeped in monarchical traditions. The immediate post-revolutionary period was characterized by political unrest and frequent changes in leadership, which created an environment of uncertainty. This instability was detrimental to economic development as it hindered long-term planning and investment. Political factions battled for control, leading to a series of short-lived governments that struggled to implement coherent economic policies.

One of the most pressing issues was the significant national debt inherited from the monarchy, exacerbated by the costs associated with maintaining the new republican government. The republic was burdened by high interest payments and the need to finance various social programs aimed at addressing the needs of a population eager for reform. The reliance on foreign loans became a recurring theme, as the government sought immediate financial relief. However, these loans often came with stringent conditions that further complicated Portugal's economic sovereignty.

Moreover, the global economic climate during the early 20th century added layers of complexity to Portugal's struggles. The repercussions of World War I were felt acutely in the Portuguese economy, particularly as the nation entered the conflict in 1916. The war strained resources and disrupted trade routes, leading to shortages of essential goods. The impacts of inflation became pronounced, as the costs of living skyrocketed, causing discontent among the populace. The government's attempts to stabilize the economy through various measures often fell short, leading to widespread strikes and social unrest. The agricultural sector, a cornerstone of the Portuguese economy, also faced dire challenges during this period. Many rural areas were impoverished, and agricultural production lagged behind other European nations. The lack of modernization in farming techniques hindered productivity, resulting in food shortages that further fueled inflation. The rural population, largely dependent on subsistence farming, found themselves caught in a cycle of debt and poverty, exacerbating social tensions.

Industrialization was another avenue that the First Republic sought to pursue; however, progress was slow. The economic policies implemented aimed to stimulate industrial growth were often poorly conceived and lacked the necessary infrastructure to support such development. Factory workers faced harsh conditions, and labor movements emerged, advocating for better wages and working conditions. The struggle between industrialists and labor unions added to the volatility of the political landscape.

The culmination of these economic struggles led to a profound crisis by the mid-1920s. In 1926, a military coup marked the end of the First Republic, as disillusionment with its economic performance and political instability reached a tipping point. The ensuing authoritarian regime sought to stabilize the economy through more centralized control, but the legacy of economic turmoil remained a poignant reminder of the challenges faced during the First Republic.

In conclusion, the economic turmoil and financial crisis of the First Republic were driven by a combination of inherited debt, political instability, the impacts of World War I, and stagnation in agricultural and industrial sectors. These factors not only shaped the immediate economic landscape but also set the stage for the eventual rise of authoritarianism in Portugal, as the populace sought stability in the face of persistent economic hardship. The lessons drawn from this period underscore the intricate relationship between political governance and economic health, a theme that resonates throughout Portugal's subsequent history.

The Downfall of the First Republic

The First Portuguese Republic, established in 1910 after the revolution that overthrew the monarchy, was marked by an ambitious agenda of modernization and democratization. However, it faced significant challenges that ultimately led to its downfall and paved the way for authoritarianism. Several interrelated factors contributed to the destabilization of the republic, including political fragmentation, economic turmoil, social unrest, and military intervention.

Political Fragmentation and Instability

From its inception, the First Republic was plagued by political fragmentation. A multitude of political parties emerged, reflecting a broad spectrum of ideologies ranging from socialist to republican and even monarchist factions. This diversity, while a sign of a vibrant political landscape, resulted in an unstable parliamentary system characterized by frequent changes in government. Between 1910 and 1926, Portugal saw 45 different governments, many of which were short-lived due to coalition breakdowns and power struggles. The inability of political leaders to form stable alliances or implement coherent policies eroded public confidence in the democratic process and governance.

Economic Turmoil

The economic landscape of Portugal during the early 20th century was equally tumultuous. The country struggled with the repercussions of World War I, which disrupted trade and exacerbated existing economic challenges. Inflation soared, and the cost of living increased dramatically, leading to widespread discontent among the working and middle classes. Economic hardship fueled strikes and protests, further destabilizing the already fragile government. The disillusionment with the republic's failure to address these pressing economic issues contributed to a growing sentiment that authoritarian rule might restore order and efficiency.

Social Unrest and Class Conflicts

Social unrest was a critical factor in the decline of the First Republic. The post-revolutionary period saw the emergence of labor movements and increased activism among workers, who were demanding better wages and working conditions. The government's inability to respond effectively to these demands led to strikes and violent confrontations. Additionally, the growing influence of radical leftist movements, including the Portuguese Communist Party, raised fears among the ruling elite and the bourgeoisie of a potential socialist revolution. This climate of fear further polarized society and pushed moderates towards authoritarian solutions as a means of restoring stability.

Military Intervention and the Rise of Authoritarianism

As political and social crises escalated, the military began to play a more prominent role in Portuguese politics. The military's growing dissatisfaction with the republic's handling of national issues, coupled with its desire for power, culminated in a series of coups and interventions. The most notable was the coup d'état of May 1926, which ultimately led to the establishment of a military dictatorship. General Gomes da Costa, who led the coup, was initially seen as a stabilizing force, but his government quickly devolved into authoritarian rule.

The rise of authoritarianism was further solidified when António de Oliveira Salazar, a finance minister, was appointed to manage the economic crisis. His technocratic approach and emphasis on order, stability, and nationalism won popular support but also set the stage for the Estado Novo regime, which would dominate Portuguese politics for decades.

Chapter 11

The Estado Novo Regime

The Rise of Salazar

António de Oliveira Salazar's ascent to power in Portugal is a pivotal event in the country's history, marking the establishment of the Estado Novo regime, a corporatist authoritarian state that would govern Portugal for nearly four decades. Salazar's rise can be attributed to a combination of historical, political, and economic factors that created a fertile ground for his authoritarian rule.

Born in 1889 in the small town of Santa Comba Dão, Salazar was educated at the University of Coimbra, where he developed a strong interest in economics and politics. His early career was marked by his work as a professor of economics, and he gained a reputation as a competent administrator. However, it was the political turmoil following the Portuguese Republican Revolution of 1910 and the subsequent instability that set the stage for his rise. The First Portuguese Republic, established after the fall of the monarchy, was characterized by frequent changes of government, social unrest, and economic difficulties, leading to widespread disillusionment among the populace.

In this context of chaos, Salazar was appointed the Minister of Finance in 1928 by President Bernardino Luís Machado Guimarães. His initial task was to restore financial stability to a nation beleaguered by debt and economic mismanagement. Salazar implemented a series of austere measures that focused on balancing the budget, reducing public spending, and stabilizing the currency. His success in achieving fiscal stability earned him significant popularity and respect among conservative factions in Portuguese society, as well as among the military.

Salazar's approach resonated with those who longed for strong leadership and a return to traditional values, which they felt had been undermined by the republican governments. His reputation as a man of integrity and competence became the cornerstone of his political identity. In 1932, Salazar was appointed Prime Minister, a position he would hold for the next 38 years. He consolidated power by avoiding elections and ruling through a mix of legal authority and coercion, effectively sidelining opposition parties.

The political landscape of the time facilitated Salazar's consolidation of power. The rise of fascism across Europe provided a model for authoritarian governance. Salazar's Estado Novo regime, established in 1933, drew inspiration from corporatism and sought to create a new order that emphasized nationalism, discipline, and social harmony. The regime's ideology was rooted in Catholic values, opposing both communism and liberalism, and it promoted the concept of a "traditional" Portuguese identity, which resonated strongly within the conservative segments of society.

To maintain control, Salazar established a secret police force, the PIDE (Polícia Internacional e de Defesa do Estado), which suppressed dissent and political opposition. The regime employed censorship and propaganda to shape public perception and stifle any form of dissent. Salazar's governance was characterized by a paternalistic approach, promoting social welfare initiatives while simultaneously curtailing civil liberties.

In foreign policy, Salazar maintained a stance of neutrality during World War II, which further solidified his position domestically as a stabilizing force. The regime capitalized on the post-war context, promoting nationalism and the idea of a Portuguese empire, albeit diminished, as a source of pride.

Salazar's rise to power was a complex interplay of effective governance, societal discontent with the prior republican regime, and the broader European political climate. His ability to present himself as a savior of the nation amidst chaos allowed him to shape Portugal's future for decades, ultimately leading to a regime that would deeply influence the country's socio-political landscape until the Carnation Revolution in 1974.

The Consolidation of the Estado Novo

The Estado Novo, or New State, was an authoritarian regime that emerged in Portugal in the early 20th century, under the leadership of António de Oliveira Salazar. Established in the aftermath of the political instability that plagued the First Portuguese Republic, the Estado Novo sought to create a stable and centralized state, marked by economic modernization, national unity, and social conservatism. The consolidation of this regime involved a multifaceted approach to governance, encompassing political repression, state propaganda, economic development, and the construction of a national identity.

Political Repression and Control

One of the regime's primary methods of consolidation was the establishment of a repressive political apparatus designed to stifle dissent and eliminate opposition. The secret police, known as the Polícia Internacional e de Defesa do Estado (PIDE), played a crucial role in maintaining the Estado Novo's authority. They employed surveillance, censorship, and intimidation tactics to suppress political opponents, dissenting intellectuals, and any form of organized resistance. The PIDE's extensive network of informants and agents enabled the regime to anticipate and quash potential uprisings. Political prisoners were common, and many were subjected to torture and harsh conditions in detention centers. The regime's ability to instill fear and suppress dissent effectively deterred opposition and allowed for the solidification of Salazar's power.

Propaganda and National Identity

In addition to repression, the Estado Novo utilized propaganda to cultivate a sense of national identity and to promote its ideals of order, discipline, and unity. The regime's propaganda machine, headed by the National Propaganda Directorate, disseminated a narrative that glorified the nation's past, particularly the Age of Discovery, while portraying the Estado Novo as the protector of traditional Portuguese values. This narrative emphasized Catholicism, rural life, and the virtues of the Portuguese people. Public ceremonies, military parades, and cultural events were orchestrated to instill a sense of pride and loyalty to the regime. The government also controlled education and the media, ensuring that only state-approved messages reached the public. By shaping the cultural landscape, the Estado Novo sought to create an obedient populace aligned with its vision of a strong and cohesive nation.

Economic Development and Corporatism

To further consolidate its power, the Estado Novo implemented policies aimed at economic development and modernization. Salazar, who had a background in economics, believed that a stable economy was fundamental to the regime's legitimacy. The regime pursued a corporatist economic model that aimed to mediate between workers and employers under state guidance, ostensibly to foster social harmony. Through the establishment of various state-sponsored organizations, the regime sought to control labor movements, suppress strikes, and promote collaboration between different sectors of the economy. This corporatist approach also extended to agriculture, where the government encouraged modernization and productivity to bolster the rural economy, which aligned with the regime's ideal of a pastoral society.

International Relations and Colonialism
The consolidation of the Estado Novo was also marked by its foreign policy, particularly regarding Portugal's colonial possessions. The regime maintained an imperial stance, emphasizing the importance of the overseas colonies in Africa and Asia. This focus on colonialism not only served to bolster national pride but also provided economic resources necessary for the regime's survival. In the face of increasing anti-colonial movements in the mid-20th century, the Estado Novo's commitment to maintaining its empire became a point of contention, leading to both internal dissent and international criticism.

In summary, the consolidation of the Estado Novo was characterized by a combination of political repression, propaganda, economic policy, and colonial ambitions. Through these mechanisms, Salazar established a regime that prioritized stability and control, while simultaneously crafting a narrative that resonated with traditional Portuguese values. The Estado Novo's legacy would profoundly impact Portugal's political landscape, leading to resistance movements that ultimately culminated in the Carnation Revolution of 1974.

Portugal's Role in World War II

During World War II, Portugal adopted a policy of neutrality that was both a strategic choice and a reflection of its historical context. The nation's neutrality was largely shaped by its long-standing alliance with Britain, the geopolitical landscape of Europe, and the internal political dynamics under the Estado Novo regime led by António de Oliveira Salazar.

Portugal's neutrality was formalized through its commitment to remain non-belligerent, a decision that was influenced by the devastation of World War I and the desire to avoid a repeat of the catastrophic consequences that had befallen many European nations. Salazar, a nationalist and authoritarian leader, believed that remaining neutral would best serve Portugal's interests, allowing the country to preserve its sovereignty and avoid the chaos that engulfed much of Europe.

The alliance with Britain, established in the Treaty of Windsor in 1386, played a crucial role in Portugal's wartime strategy. As the war progressed, the British were keen to maintain good relations with Portugal, seeing it as a strategic ally on the Iberian Peninsula. This alliance facilitated the use of Portuguese ports by British naval forces for resupply and repairs, which was vital for maintaining their presence in the Atlantic. The Azores, in particular, became a focal point for Allied operations, leading to a diplomatic agreement that allowed British military access to these islands in 1943.

Despite its neutrality, Portugal was not entirely insulated from the war's effects. The country became a haven for refugees fleeing the conflict, particularly Jews escaping Nazi persecution. Lisbon, in particular, emerged as a significant transit point for those seeking to flee to the Americas. Portuguese consuls, notably Aristides de Sousa Mendes, played a heroic role by issuing visas to thousands of refugees, often against the directives of the Salazar government, highlighting the complexities of Portugal's wartime position.

Economically, Portugal benefited from its neutrality. The nation continued to trade with both the Axis and Allied powers, exporting valuable goods such as tungsten, a critical material for the production of armaments. This trade not only bolstered the Portuguese economy but also provided the regime with the financial resources necessary to maintain its grip on power. The duality of this trade relationship exemplified the pragmatic approach of Salazar's government, which sought to maximize Portugal's economic benefits while minimizing involvement in the conflict.

Salazar's regime also faced internal challenges during the war. The political landscape was marked by the need to suppress dissent and maintain control over a population that was increasingly aware of the wider implications of the conflict. The regime utilized censorship and propaganda to promote its narrative of neutrality and stability, emphasizing the dangers of communism and the need for a strong authoritarian government to preserve national unity.

As the war drew to a close, Portugal's neutrality allowed it to emerge relatively unscathed compared to its European neighbors. However, the end of the war marked a turning point for Portugal. The nation faced pressure to align more closely with the emerging post-war order, including the decolonization movements in Africa and Asia. Salazar's regime, while initially resistant, would have to confront the geopolitical realities of a world reshaped by the war.

In summary, Portugal's role during World War II was characterized by a complex interplay of neutrality, economic pragmatism, and diplomatic maneuvering. The Estado Novo regime's strategic decisions allowed Portugal to navigate the tumultuous waters of the war while preserving its sovereignty and economic interests, albeit at the cost of moral complicity in the face of global conflict.

The PIDE and Political Repression

The PIDE, or Polícia Internacional e de Defesa do Estado, was the secret police of Portugal during the Estado Novo regime, which lasted from 1933 until the Carnation Revolution in 1974. Established in 1945, PIDE was a critical instrument in the authoritarian government led by António de Oliveira Salazar and later by Marcello Caetano. Its primary purpose was to maintain the regime's stability by suppressing dissent, controlling political opposition, and instilling fear among the populace.

The emergence of PIDE was rooted in the broader context of the Estado Novo, which sought to create a corporatist state characterized by nationalism, conservatism, and a rejection of liberal democracy. Salazar's government viewed political dissent as a threat to national unity and social order, leading to the establishment of a surveillance apparatus designed to monitor and control the population. PIDE operated under the justification of protecting the state from internal and external threats, particularly communism and any revolutionary ideologies that could destabilize the regime.

PIDE's methods of repression were extensive and insidious. It employed a range of tactics including surveillance, infiltration of opposition groups, arbitrary arrests, and torture. Agents of PIDE would infiltrate labor unions, student organizations, and any groups that showed signs of dissent. This allowed them to gather intelligence and dismantle opposition before it could gain traction. The fear of being watched created a climate of self-censorship among the general populace, stifling free expression and dissenting voices.

Interrogation techniques employed by PIDE were notorious for their brutality. Detainees often faced physical and psychological torture, with reports of beatings, electric shocks, and isolation being common. This not only served to extract confessions but also to instill fear across society. PIDE utilized these tactics not just to punish individuals but to create a pervasive atmosphere of intimidation that discouraged any thoughts of rebellion or resistance.

The PIDE also played a crucial role in the regime's propaganda efforts. By controlling the narrative surrounding political dissent, they sought to portray opponents of the Estado Novo as subversive elements threatening the fabric of Portuguese society. The regime utilized media censorship to shape public perception, and PIDE was instrumental in silencing dissenting journalists and intellectuals who might challenge the official line.

Despite its efforts, the repressive measures of the PIDE ultimately sowed the seeds of discontent. As the economic and social conditions in Portugal began to deteriorate, dissatisfaction with the regime grew. Activists, intellectuals, and members of the military began to coalesce around a vision for a democratic Portugal, leading to the formation of clandestine groups that sought to undermine PIDE's authority.

The culmination of this resistance occurred during the Carnation Revolution on April 25, 1974. The military coup, supported by widespread popular discontent and nonviolent protests, led to the overthrow of the Estado Novo regime. PIDE's power crumbled rapidly as soldiers and civilians took to the streets, symbolized by the red carnations worn by revolutionaries.

In the aftermath, the PIDE was disbanded, and its leaders were arrested or fled the country. The legacy of PIDE's repression left deep scars on Portuguese society, contributing to a collective memory of fear and oppression. The transition to democracy required not only political reform but also a reckoning with the human rights abuses that had occurred under the regime. In contemporary Portugal, the history of the PIDE serves as a reminder of the importance of safeguarding democratic values and human rights against the backdrop of authoritarianism. The lessons learned from this dark chapter continue to shape Portugal's political landscape and its commitment to civil liberties.

The Fall of the Estado Novo

The Estado Novo regime, established by António de Oliveira Salazar in 1933, was characterized by an authoritarian governance structure that emphasized nationalism, corporatism, and a strong Catholic influence. Initially, Salazar's regime enjoyed a degree of stability, but by the 1960s, various socio-political and economic factors began to erode its foundation, ultimately culminating in the Carnation Revolution of April 25, 1974.

One of the primary factors contributing to the fall of the Estado Novo was the regime's inability to adapt to changing societal dynamics. Throughout the 1960s, Portugal was marked by increasing discontent among various segments of the population. The economic policies of the Estado Novo, which emphasized agriculture and traditional industries, failed to meet the demands of a growing urban population. While Portugal experienced some economic growth post-World War II, the benefits were unevenly distributed, leading to significant disparities that fueled social unrest. The working class, particularly in urban centers, became increasingly frustrated with stagnant wages and poor living conditions, leading to strikes and demonstrations.

The regime's colonial wars in Africa also played a crucial role in its decline. From the early 1960s onward, Portugal was embroiled in protracted conflicts in its African colonies, including Angola, Mozambique, and Guinea-Bissau. These wars not only drained Portugal's resources but also became increasingly unpopular among the Portuguese populace. The regime's insistence on maintaining its colonial empire clashed with the rising tide of anti-colonial sentiment both domestically and globally. As the wars dragged on, they resulted in significant casualties and economic strain, leading to widespread disillusionment with the Estado Novo.

Moreover, the repressive nature of the regime, enforced by the secret police (PIDE), contributed to growing opposition. The PIDE's brutal tactics stifled dissent but also fostered a culture of fear and resentment. Political prisoners and censorship were commonplace, and the lack of political freedoms drove many intellectuals, artists, and students to oppose the regime. The emergence of underground movements and political organizations, such as the Portuguese Communist Party and the Armed Forces Movement (MFA), signaled the growing discontent and the desire for change.
Internationally, the context of the Cold War also affected the Estado Novo. Portugal was increasingly isolated, particularly as the decolonization movements gained momentum in Africa and Asia. The regime's alignment with the United States during the Cold War put it at odds with revolutionary movements in those regions, further alienating Portugal from the global community. The increasing

visibility of democratic movements in neighboring countries, especially the 1974 Carnation Revolution in Greece and the transition to democracy in Spain, inspired Portuguese citizens and highlighted the potential for change.

The culmination of these internal and external pressures came to a head on April 25, 1974, when the MFA, composed mainly of disillusioned military officers, orchestrated a nearly bloodless coup against the Estado Novo. The revolution was marked by the iconic use of carnations as symbols of peace and change, as soldiers and civilians united to overthrow the regime. The coup was met with widespread support from the populace, signaling an overwhelming desire for democratic governance and an end to decades of authoritarian rule.

Chapter 12

The Carnation Revolution

The Military Coup of April 25, 1974

The Military Coup of April 25, 1974, known as the Carnation Revolution, marked a pivotal moment in Portuguese history, leading to the overthrow of the authoritarian Estado Novo regime and the establishment of a democratic government. This non-violent coup was characterized by the unexpected collaboration between military factions and civilian supporters, culminating in a significant shift in the political landscape of Portugal.

The Estado Novo regime, led by António de Oliveira Salazar and later by Marcello Caetano, had ruled Portugal since the 1930s. The regime was marked by political repression, censorship, and a lack of civil liberties, which fostered widespread dissent among various sectors of society. By the early 1970s, Portugal faced multifaceted crises: a protracted colonial war in Africa, economic stagnation, and growing discontent among the populace. These elements contributed to a ripe environment for change, as many citizens yearned for democracy and an end to colonial conflicts.

The coup was primarily orchestrated by the Armed Forces Movement (Movimento das Forças Armadas, MFA), a group of military officers who were disillusioned with the regime's policies and the ongoing colonial wars in Angola, Mozambique, and Guinea-Bissau. The MFA was composed of progressive officers, many of whom had fought in the colonial wars and returned deeply affected by their experiences. They sought to end the wars, restore democracy, and implement social reforms.

On the evening of April 24, 1974, the MFA initiated its plan, which was codenamed "Operation Ghost." The coup began with a series of coordinated actions, including the strategic occupation of key military installations in Lisbon and other major cities. The coup leaders understood that controlling communication channels was essential for their success. Therefore, they seized the radio stations and broadcast messages calling for the end of the Estado Novo regime.

Amidst a backdrop of uncertainty, the coup's first major success came when thousands of citizens took to the streets in support of the military. The symbolic use of red carnations, which were handed out by soldiers to civilians, became a powerful emblem of the revolution. This peaceful exchange between the military and the populace underscored the coup's non-violent nature and the desire for change without bloodshed.

As the morning of April 25 unfolded, thousands of protesting citizens began to gather in Lisbon, demanding an end to the dictatorship. The military's advance was met with minimal resistance, as many loyalist troops either defected to the MFA or refused to engage in a violent confrontation. Notably, Marcello Caetano, the then-leader of Portugal, was taken by surprise and sought refuge in the São Bento Palace. Eventually, he surrendered to the MFA, marking the regime's collapse.

By the end of the day, the Carnation Revolution had effectively dismantled the Estado Novo regime. The MFA formed a provisional government to oversee the transition to democracy. The revolution was celebrated not only as a military success but also as a triumph of the Portuguese people who had long endured oppression.

In the aftermath, Portugal experienced a wave of political activity, including the decolonization of Africa and the establishment of a democratic constitution in 1976. The Carnation Revolution remains a defining moment in Portugal's history, symbolizing the profound desire for freedom and democracy, and its legacy continues to influence Portuguese society and politics to this day.

The Role of the MFA and Its Impact on the Revolution

The Armed Forces Movement (Movimento das Forças Armadas, MFA) was a pivotal force in the Carnation Revolution of April 25, 1974, which ultimately led to the fall of the Estado Novo regime in Portugal. The MFA was composed of military officers who were disillusioned with the authoritarian regime of António de Oliveira Salazar and his successor, Marcelo Caetano. These officers recognized the need for change not only within the military but also in the broader political landscape of Portugal, which had been marked by repression, censorship, and a protracted colonial war in Africa.

The origins of the MFA can be traced back to the dissatisfaction within the Portuguese military, particularly among younger officers who had been exposed to international ideals of democracy and freedom during their service in Africa. The protracted colonial wars in Angola, Mozambique, and Guinea-Bissau, which began in the early 1960s, drained resources and morale and highlighted the shortcomings of the Estado Novo regime. Many military personnel believed that the continuation of these wars was unjust and unsustainable. This sentiment fostered a growing desire for political change among the ranks.

In the early 1970s, a core group of military officers began to organize and lay the groundwork for a revolution. They created secret networks to discuss their grievances and plan for a possible coup. The MFA was formally established in 1974, with the intent of overthrowing the government and restoring democracy in Portugal. Its members were motivated by a combination of political ideals, a commitment to national sovereignty, and a desire to end the colonial wars.

The revolution itself began early on the morning of April 25, 1974, when MFA members executed a well-coordinated coup. They took control of key military installations and strategic points in Lisbon, the capital, while also cutting off communications to minimize the government's ability to respond. The operation was remarkably efficient, and within hours, the MFA had effectively seized power with minimal bloodshed. The iconic image of the revolution is that of soldiers and civilians alike placing red carnations in the barrels of rifles—a symbol of peace and a stark contrast to the violence that had characterized the Estado Novo regime.

The impact of the MFA on the revolution was profound. The movement not only catalyzed the overthrow of the Estado Novo but also played a crucial role in shaping the political landscape of post-revolutionary Portugal. After the success of the coup, the MFA took control of the government and initiated a series of reforms aimed at dismantling the authoritarian structures that had long dominated Portuguese life. They established a transitional government that prioritized civil liberties, political pluralism, and the decolonization of Portuguese territories in Africa.

The MFA also faced significant challenges as it sought to navigate the complexities of power and governance in a rapidly changing political environment. The organization was not a monolith; it encompassed a range of political ideologies, from moderate socialists to radical leftists. This diversity of views sometimes led to internal conflicts and disagreements about the direction of the new government.

Despite these challenges, the MFA's commitment to democratization was instrumental in laying the groundwork for a new constitutional order. The revolution inspired a wave of political engagement among the Portuguese populace, leading to the establishment of political parties, the drafting of a new constitution in 1976, and the eventual consolidation of democracy in Portugal.

In conclusion, the MFA played a crucial role in the Carnation Revolution, serving as the catalyst for change that ended decades of authoritarian rule. Its impact extended far beyond the immediate overthrow of the Estado Novo regime, as it facilitated Portugal's transition to democracy and the decolonization of its African territories, forever altering the trajectory of Portuguese history. The legacy of the MFA remains a vital part of Portugal's national identity and democratic values today.

Decolonization and the End of the Empire

The decolonization of Portugal's overseas empire, which spanned several continents and included territories in Africa, Asia, and South America, was a complex and tumultuous process that unfolded primarily during the mid-20th century. This period was marked by significant political, social, and economic upheaval, both within Portugal and in its colonies. The culmination of these events led to the dismantling of Portugal's empire, a long-standing global power structure that had lasted for centuries.

The roots of decolonization can be traced back to the rise of nationalist movements within the Portuguese colonies. After World War II, there was a global wave of decolonization spurred by the principles of self-determination and the weakening of European powers. In Africa, nationalist movements began to gain traction as local leaders and populations sought to assert their identity and autonomy. Countries such as Angola, Mozambique, and Guinea-Bissau became focal points for liberation struggles, with various groups forming to combat Portuguese colonial rule. The African Party for the Independence of Guinea and Cape Verde (PAIGC), the Popular Movement for the Liberation of Angola (MPLA), and the Mozambique Liberation Front (FRELIMO) emerged as key players in these struggles.

Simultaneously, Portugal was experiencing its own political turmoil under the Estado Novo regime, an authoritarian government that resisted calls for reform and independence. The regime's refusal to acknowledge the growing discontent and demands for independence from its colonies led to a prolonged and violent response. Portugal's military involvement in Africa became increasingly costly and unpopular, especially as casualties mounted and the war effort strained national resources.

The turning point for Portugal came with the Carnation Revolution on April 25, 1974. This non-violent coup, led by a group of military officers known as the Armed Forces Movement (MFA), aimed to overthrow the oppressive Estado Novo regime. The revolution was characterized by its peaceful nature, symbolized by the red carnations worn by the revolutionaries. The success of the coup led to a significant shift in Portuguese policy regarding its colonies. Within a few months of the revolution, the new government recognized the urgency of decolonization and began negotiating with liberation movements.

Negotiations led to a rapid decolonization process. The first significant territory to gain independence was Guinea-Bissau in 1973, which was followed by Mozambique (1975), Angola (1975), and Cape Verde (1975). The speed of this process was unprecedented and marked a stark contrast to the protracted conflicts that preceded it. The new Portuguese government recognized that maintaining the empire was no longer feasible, both politically and economically.

The consequences of decolonization were profound, impacting both Portugal and the newly independent nations. For Portugal, the loss of its empire meant a dramatic shift in its global standing and economic viability. The once-thriving colonial economy collapsed, leading to economic reorientation and challenges in integrating returning soldiers and settlers who had lived in the colonies. This transition prompted a reevaluation of national identity and purpose.

For the newly independent nations, the struggle for self-governance was just beginning. The legacies of colonialism, including economic dependency, social fragmentation, and political instability, posed significant challenges. In Angola, for example, the power vacuum following independence led to a brutal civil war that lasted until 2002, exacerbating the difficulties faced by the newly established state.

In conclusion, the decolonization of Portugal's overseas empire was a pivotal moment in both Portuguese and global history. It not only marked the end of a colonial era that had lasted for centuries but also initiated a complex process of nation-building and identity formation in the liberated territories. The impact of these historical shifts continues to resonate in contemporary post-colonial relationships and the socio-political landscape of both Portugal and its former colonies.

Social and Economic Changes Post-Revolution

The Carnation Revolution of April 25, 1974, marked a significant turning point in Portuguese history, leading to profound social and economic transformations that reshaped the nation. The overthrow of the Estado Novo regime, which had been characterized by authoritarianism and repression, opened the door to a new era of democracy, civil liberties, and economic reform.

In the immediate aftermath of the revolution, there was a surge of enthusiasm for change among the Portuguese populace. Citizens who had long been stifled by censorship and political oppression began to engage actively in democratic processes. Political participation soared as new political parties emerged, and citizens exercised their right to vote in free elections for the first time in decades. This democratization fostered a climate of political pluralism and social activism, empowering previously marginalized groups, including women, workers, and youth, who began to advocate for their rights and interests.

Socially, the revolution catalyzed a wave of progressive reforms. Land reform was one of the most significant initiatives, as the new government sought to dismantle the large estates held by the elite and redistribute land to small farmers. The Agrarian Reform Movement aimed to increase agricultural productivity and reduce rural poverty, although it faced challenges such as resistance from landowners and inefficiencies in management. Nonetheless, these reforms aimed to empower the rural population and promote greater social equity.

Urban areas also experienced transformative changes. The state adopted policies aimed at improving housing and public services, addressing the housing crisis that had plagued many cities. Public investment in infrastructure led to the construction of new schools, hospitals, and transportation networks, which improved the quality of life for many citizens. The emphasis on education was particularly notable, as literacy rates began to rise dramatically, laying the foundation for a more informed and engaged citizenry.

Economically, the revolution ushered in a period of restructuring and modernization. The government nationalized key industries, including banking, transportation, and telecommunications, with the aim of reducing foreign control over the economy and promoting national interests. This shift was designed to create a more equitable economic environment, although it also led to inefficiencies and bureaucratic challenges. While nationalization aimed to protect workers' rights and enhance social welfare, it often resulted in economic stagnation and limited foreign investment.

The integration into the European Economic Community (EEC) in 1986 marked another pivotal moment for Portugal's economy. This accession facilitated access to European markets and development funds, spurring significant economic growth and modernization. The influx of EEC funds enabled substantial investments in infrastructure, education, and industry, contributing to an economic boom in the late 1980s and early 1990s. This period saw an increase in foreign investment, the expansion of the tourism sector, and the emergence of a vibrant service economy.

However, these changes were not without challenges. The rapid economic growth led to increasing disparities between urban and rural areas, as well as between different regions of the country. Economic crises, particularly during the late 2000s and early 2010s, exposed vulnerabilities in the Portuguese economy, leading to austerity measures and social unrest. The Eurozone crisis had a profound impact, resulting in high unemployment rates and public discontent.

In summary, the social and economic changes in Portugal following the Carnation Revolution were marked by a shift towards democracy, social equity, and economic modernization. While these changes brought about significant progress and opportunities, they also highlighted ongoing challenges that required continuous adaptation and reform. The legacy of the revolution continues to influence Portuguese society and its economic landscape, shaping the nation's trajectory as it navigates the complexities of the 21st century.

The Establishment of Democracy in Post-Revolution Portugal

The Carnation Revolution of April 25, 1974, marked a pivotal moment in Portugal's history, leading to the establishment of a democratic government after nearly five decades of authoritarian rule under the Estado Novo regime. The revolution was characterized by a nearly bloodless military coup, spearheaded by the Armed Forces Movement (Movimento das Forças Armadas, MFA), which sought to end the oppressive regime and restore civil liberties to the Portuguese people. The immediate aftermath of the revolution set the stage for a complex and transformative process towards democracy.

Initially, following the revolution, Portugal was governed by a National Salvation Junta, which was a provisional governing body composed primarily of military leaders. This junta was tasked with managing the transition from dictatorship to democracy, and it quickly moved to dismantle the repressive structures of the Estado Novo. Political prisoners were released, censorship was lifted, and political parties were legalized, including the Portuguese Communist Party and the Socialist Party. This pluralistic environment led to a flourishing of political discourse and activism as the Portuguese sought to redefine their national identity and governance.

The first major step towards a democratic government was the establishment of the Constitutional Assembly in 1975. This body was responsible for drafting a new constitution that would enshrine democratic principles, human rights, and the rule of law. The assembly comprised representatives from various political parties, reflecting the diverse ideologies and aspirations of the post-revolutionary society. After extensive debates and deliberations, the new Constitution of Portugal was promulgated on April 2, 1976. It marked a significant milestone in the country's transition, establishing Portugal as a democratic republic with a clear commitment to social justice, equality, and the protection of individual liberties.

The constitution enshrined fundamental rights, including freedom of expression, assembly, and association, and it laid the groundwork for a parliamentary democracy, with a system of checks and balances among the executive, legislative, and judicial branches. The first democratic elections for the Assembly of the Republic took place in April 1976, culminating in a victory for the Socialist Party, which was led by Mário Soares. Soares became the first democratically elected Prime Minister of Portugal, marking a shift from military governance to civilian rule.

Despite the optimism surrounding the establishment of democracy, the transition was not without challenges. The early years of the democratic regime were marked by political instability, economic difficulties, and conflicts between various political factions. The country faced the legacy of the colonial wars in Africa, which had left deep societal scars and complicated the process of nation-building. Moreover, the polarization of the political landscape often led to tensions between leftist and rightist factions, as well as between moderate and radical elements within the political system.

To address these challenges, the new government undertook significant economic and social reforms aimed at modernizing the economy and integrating previously marginalized communities. Nationalization of key industries and land reform were implemented to redistribute wealth and empower the lower classes. However, these policies also faced criticism for their speed and effectiveness, leading to further political contention.

Over time, the consolidation of democracy in Portugal became more stable. The country's integration into the European Economic Community (EEC) in 1986 provided a framework for economic development and political stability. EU membership facilitated investment and modernization, which contributed to the strengthening of democratic institutions and the rule of law.

By the turn of the century, Portugal had firmly established itself as a democratic state, characterized by regular elections, a vibrant civil society, and a commitment to European integration. The journey from dictatorship to democracy in Portugal serves as a testament to the resilience of its people and the enduring importance of civic engagement in shaping a nation's future.

Chapter 13

Portugal in the European Union

Portugal's Path to EU Membership

The journey of Portugal towards European Union (EU) membership is a significant chapter in the nation's modern history, reflecting its quest for political stability, economic development, and deeper integration into Europe following decades of dictatorship. The groundwork for Portugal's EU membership was laid in the aftermath of the Carnation Revolution of 1974, which ended the Estado Novo regime and ushered in a new era of democracy.

1. Political Transformation Post-Revolution

The Carnation Revolution not only liberated Portugal from authoritarian rule but also stimulated a desire for modernization and alignment with Western Europe. The new democratic government recognized the importance of joining the European movement as a means to secure political stability and economic assistance. The early years of democracy saw Portugal restructuring its political institutions and embracing European ideals of governance, human rights, and the rule of law, which were essential prerequisites for EU membership.

2. Application for Membership

In 1977, the Portuguese government formally applied for accession to the European Economic Community (EEC), which was the precursor to the EU. This application was motivated by the need for economic recovery and development following years of isolation and colonial wars. The EEC represented an opportunity for Portugal to access new markets, attract foreign investment, and benefit from regional development funds. However, the application process was complex, requiring significant reforms and alignment with EEC standards.

3. Negotiation Phase

The negotiations for Portugal's membership commenced in 1979, alongside Spain's application. Both countries faced the dual challenge of meeting the economic criteria set by the EEC and managing their domestic political landscapes. The EEC's requirements included economic stabilization, democratic governance, and adherence to common policies, particularly in agriculture and fisheries, which were vital sectors in the Portuguese economy. The negotiations were marked by a commitment to reform and modernization, which included agricultural adjustments and industrial competitiveness.

4. Economic Adjustments

Portugal's economy required substantial restructuring to meet EEC standards. The government implemented various reforms aimed at liberalizing trade, improving fiscal policies, and enhancing productivity. The EEC recognized the economic challenges faced by Portugal, particularly its lower economic development compared to other member states. Consequently, the EEC proposed a transitional period of financial aid and support to facilitate Portugal's integration into the community. This included significant investments in infrastructure, education, and economic diversification.

5. Final Accession

On January 1, 1986, Portugal officially became a member of the European Economic Community, alongside Spain. The accession was celebrated as a historic milestone, marking the end of a long journey towards integration with Western Europe. Membership opened the doors to the single market, allowing Portugal to benefit from free movement of goods, services, and capital. The country received substantial funding through various EEC programs, which catalyzed economic growth and development.

6. Impact of Membership

Joining the EEC transformed Portugal's economic landscape, leading to increased foreign direct investment and modernization of key industries. It also reinforced democratic governance and political stability, fostering a sense of belonging within the European family. Over the years, Portugal adapted to EU policies and regulations, which further strengthened its institutions and governance.

In conclusion, Portugal's path to EU membership was a multifaceted process marked by significant political and economic transformations. The journey from dictatorship to democracy, coupled with the commitment to reform and integration, not only facilitated Portugal's accession to the EEC but also shaped its trajectory as a modern European nation in the decades that followed.

The Impact of EU Membership

Portugal's accession to the European Union (EU) in 1986 marked a pivotal moment in its modern history, fundamentally reshaping the nation's economic and political landscape. The integration into the EU framework not only provided Portugal with access to substantial financial resources but also facilitated significant reforms that transformed various sectors of the economy and governance.

Economic Transformation and Growth

One of the most immediate impacts of EU membership was the injection of funds through the European Structural and Investment Funds. These financial resources were instrumental in modernizing Portugal's infrastructure, including transportation, telecommunications, and energy sectors. Major projects, such as the construction of the A1 motorway and the expansion of Lisbon's airport, were made possible through EU funding, which greatly enhanced connectivity and accessibility.

The integration into the single market allowed Portugal to benefit from increased trade and investment opportunities. Portuguese exports saw a significant rise, particularly in agricultural products, textiles, and electronics, as local businesses gained access to a broader European market. This shift contributed to an overall economic growth rate that was above the EU average during the 1990s and early 2000s, ultimately leading to a diversification of the economy away from traditional sectors.

Social and Labor Market Reforms

EU membership prompted Portugal to align its labor laws and social policies with European standards, fostering improvements in workers' rights and protections. The adoption of directives on health and safety at work, anti-discrimination measures, and labor market regulations helped create a more equitable and stable working environment. As a result, Portugal witnessed an increase in labor force participation, particularly among women, which contributed to economic development and social cohesion.

Additionally, Portugal benefited from educational and training programs funded by the EU, such as the European Social Fund. These initiatives aimed to enhance skills and employability, addressing unemployment, particularly among youth. The emphasis on education and vocational training has had lasting effects on the labor market, enabling a more skilled workforce capable of meeting the demands of a modern economy.

Political Influence and Democratic Maturity

Politically, EU membership reinforced democratic governance in Portugal. The requirement for adherence to EU democratic norms and principles encouraged the strengthening of institutions and the rule of law. The EU's role in promoting transparency, accountability, and good governance has been vital in consolidating Portugal's democracy, particularly following the authoritarian Estado Novo regime that lasted until the mid-20th century.

Moreover, Portugal's participation in EU decision-making processes has allowed it to amplify its influence on the international stage. By being part of a larger bloc, Portugal has been able to advocate for its interests, particularly in areas like agricultural policy and regional development, which are crucial for its economy. The Portuguese government has also benefited from EU diplomatic support in various international forums, enhancing its global presence.

Challenges and Economic Crisis

Despite the benefits, Portugal's EU membership has not been without challenges. The global financial crisis of 2008 and the subsequent Eurozone crisis put significant strain on the Portuguese economy and highlighted vulnerabilities within its fiscal and economic frameworks. The austerity measures imposed by the EU and the International Monetary Fund (IMF) in exchange for financial assistance led to widespread public discontent and social unrest. These measures, while aimed at fiscal stabilization, often exacerbated socio-economic inequalities and challenged the fabric of Portuguese society.

In conclusion, Portugal's EU membership has profoundly influenced its economic and political landscape, driving modernization, growth, and democratic consolidation. While the journey has included significant challenges, the overall impact of EU integration has been transformative, positioning Portugal as a key player within the European framework and shaping its future in a rapidly changing global environment. As Portugal continues to navigate contemporary challenges, the lessons learned from its EU experience will remain essential in guiding its path forward.

Portugal's Role in European Politics

Portugal's engagement in European politics has evolved significantly since it became a member of the European Union (EU) in 1986. This accession marked a pivotal moment in Portuguese history, transforming the nation from a relatively isolated state recovering from decades of dictatorship into an active participant in European affairs. The integration into the EU provided Portugal with not only economic opportunities but also a platform to influence regional policies and foster international relationships.

One of the most significant aspects of Portugal's EU membership has been its involvement in shaping and benefiting from EU policies. The country has been a strong advocate for cohesion and solidarity within the EU framework. As one of the less economically robust member states, Portugal has consistently pushed for policies aimed at reducing disparities among EU nations. This advocacy is particularly evident in the context of regional development funds, which have facilitated substantial investment in infrastructure and social programs across Portugal, helping to modernize the country and improve living conditions.

Portugal has also played an active role in promoting the EU's values, such as democracy, human rights, and the rule of law. The nation has historically supported the enlargement of the EU, advocating for the inclusion of Eastern European countries following the fall of the Iron Curtain. This stance reflects Portugal's own historical experiences with authoritarianism and its commitment to fostering democratic governance within Europe. By supporting the integration of new member states, Portugal has positioned itself as a bridge between Western and Eastern Europe, fostering cooperation and mutual understanding.

In terms of foreign policy, Portugal has emphasized the importance of a unified EU stance on global issues. The country has been a proponent of the Common Foreign and Security Policy (CFSP), arguing for a coordinated approach to international relations that reflects the collective interests of EU member states. Portugal's historical ties with former colonies in Africa, Asia, and South America have informed its contributions to discussions on development aid and humanitarian assistance. The country has often called for the EU to take a leadership role in addressing global challenges, including climate change, migration, and security threats.

Portugal's influence within the EU has been evident through its participation in key negotiations and leadership roles. Notably, Portuguese politicians have held significant positions within EU institutions, including the presidency of the European Commission and the European Parliament. These roles have allowed Portugal to advocate for its national interests while also promoting broader European goals. The country has utilized its presidency of the Council of the European Union to address pressing issues such as economic recovery, migration, and environmental sustainability.

However, Portugal has also faced challenges in its European political landscape, particularly during the Eurozone crisis that began in 2009. The economic turmoil necessitated a bailout from the EU and the International Monetary Fund, leading to austerity measures that sparked domestic unrest and impacted Portugal's public perception of the EU. While the crisis tested the resilience of the Portuguese economy, it also served as a learning experience, emphasizing the need for deeper economic integration and fiscal responsibility within the EU.

In recent years, Portugal has emerged as a key advocate for progressive policies, such as climate action and social rights, within the EU framework. The country has positioned itself as a model for sustainable development, particularly in terms of renewable energy. Portugal's initiatives in this area have not only contributed to the EU's overall environmental goals but have also enhanced its reputation as a leader in addressing climate change.

In conclusion, Portugal's role in European politics is characterized by its commitment to cooperation, advocacy for cohesion, and active participation in shaping EU policies. The nation has navigated challenges while leveraging its strategic position to influence regional and global affairs, reflecting its transformation from a historically isolated state to a vital contributor to the European project. As Portugal continues to evolve, its voice within the EU will undoubtedly remain significant in promoting unity, sustainability, and shared prosperity.

Social Changes in Modern Portugal

In recent decades, Portugal has undergone significant social transformations, influenced by globalization and its integration into the European Union (EU). These changes have reshaped various aspects of Portuguese life, including demographics, cultural identity, economic structure, and social policy.

Demographic Changes

One of the most notable social changes in modern Portugal has been its demographic evolution. The country has seen increased immigration from various parts of the world, particularly from former colonies such as Angola, Mozambique, and Brazil, as well as from Eastern European countries. This influx has contributed to a more diverse society, enriching the cultural fabric of Portugal. Immigrants have played a crucial role in revitalizing urban areas, contributing to economic sectors like construction, hospitality, and services, which faced labor shortages.

Additionally, there has been a notable trend of emigration among young Portuguese, especially during economic downturns, such as the Eurozone crisis. Many young professionals have sought opportunities abroad, which has led to a brain drain that challenges Portugal's long-term economic prospects. However, this dual phenomenon of immigration and emigration has created a dynamic and evolving demographic landscape, fostering multiculturalism while also presenting challenges in social integration and cohesion.

Cultural Identity

Globalization has also influenced Portuguese cultural identity. The exposure to diverse cultures has led to a greater acceptance of multiculturalism, but it has also sparked debates about national identity and cultural preservation. Portuguese cuisine, music, and arts have absorbed international influences, leading to a vibrant fusion of traditional and contemporary expressions. For instance, the popularity of fusions such as "fusion cuisine" highlights the blending of global tastes with traditional Portuguese flavors.

Moreover, the role of the Portuguese language as a global language has been emphasized through cultural exchanges and the diaspora. The promotion of Portuguese culture abroad, supported by the government and cultural institutions, has helped maintain a sense of national pride while embracing global influences.

Economic Structure and Social Policy

Portugal's EU membership has catalyzed significant economic and social reforms. The adoption of EU policies and funding has accelerated modernization in various sectors, including infrastructure, education, and social services. The

EU's structural funds have financed numerous projects aimed at regional development, enhancing connectivity and living standards across the country.

Socially, EU membership has aligned Portugal with European standards regarding human rights, gender equality, and environmental sustainability. The introduction of social protection measures and labor rights has improved the quality of life for many citizens. However, challenges remain, particularly in addressing inequalities and ensuring that the benefits of globalization and EU integration reach all segments of society.

Impact of the Eurozone Crisis

The Eurozone crisis (2009-2014) had profound implications for Portuguese society. Austerity measures imposed by the EU and International Monetary Fund led to widespread social discontent, prompting protests and a rise in public activism. The crisis exposed existing inequalities and vulnerabilities within Portuguese society, leading to increased calls for social justice and economic reform. In response, the government has sought to create a more inclusive society by enhancing social safety nets and promoting equality.

Conclusion

In summary, the effects of globalization and EU membership on Portuguese society have been multifaceted, leading to demographic shifts, cultural evolution, economic modernization, and social reforms. While these changes have brought opportunities and enriched the national landscape, they have also posed challenges that require ongoing attention and adaptation. As Portugal navigates the complexities of a globalized world, its ability to balance tradition with modernity will be crucial in shaping a cohesive and resilient society for future generations.

The Eurozone Crisis and Recovery

The Eurozone crisis, which erupted in late 2009, exposed the vulnerabilities of several European economies, Portugal being one of the most affected. The crisis stemmed from a combination of high public debt levels, banking sector weaknesses, and an economic environment characterized by low growth. Portugal's economic troubles had roots that extended back to the global financial crisis of 2007-2008, which had already strained its economy. By 2010, Portugal faced a significant fiscal imbalance, with a budget deficit exceeding the

EU's threshold of 3% of GDP, and a public debt that had soared to over 90% of GDP.

In April 2011, in response to mounting pressure from financial markets and the risk of default, the Portuguese government requested a bailout from the European Union and the International Monetary Fund (IMF). The resulting financial package amounted to €78 billion, which was accompanied by stringent austerity measures aimed at restoring financial stability. These measures included cuts to public spending, tax hikes, and labor market reforms, which were deeply unpopular among the populace and led to widespread protests. The austerity measures, while necessary for fiscal consolidation, severely impacted the social fabric of the country, resulting in high unemployment rates, particularly among the youth, and a decline in living standards for many Portuguese citizens.

Despite the challenges posed by austerity, Portugal began to gradually show signs of economic recovery around 2013. The combination of internal reforms, an improving external environment, and the commitment to the bailout program were crucial in stabilizing the economy. The Portuguese government undertook significant structural reforms in various sectors, including public administration, labor markets, and the judicial system. These reforms aimed to enhance competitiveness, increase efficiency, and attract foreign investment.

Moreover, Portugal benefitted from a rebound in exports, particularly in the tourism sector, which became a key driver of growth. The country's unique cultural heritage, beautiful landscapes, and favorable climate made it an attractive destination for international travelers. By focusing on tourism and export-oriented industries, Portugal was able to diversify its economy away from the traditional reliance on domestic consumption.

In 2014, Portugal successfully exited the bailout program, a significant milestone that marked the beginning of a new chapter for the nation. The exit was celebrated as a testament to the resilience and determination of the Portuguese people, despite the sacrifices made during the austerity period. Economic indicators reflected a positive trend, with GDP growth returning to positive territory and unemployment rates starting to decline.

The recovery continued into the following years, driven by a mix of fiscal discipline and renewed confidence in the Portuguese economy. By 2017, Portugal was experiencing one of the fastest growth rates in the Eurozone, with improvements in public finances and a drop in the budget deficit to below 3% of GDP. The country's commitment to reform and stabilization was recognized by international financial institutions, leading to increased investor confidence and a resurgence in foreign direct investment.

In conclusion, while the Eurozone crisis presented significant challenges for Portugal, it also catalyzed necessary reforms that contributed to an eventual recovery. The nation emerged from the crisis with a more resilient economy, improved fiscal health, and a renewed focus on sustainable growth. The lessons learned during this tumultuous period continue to shape Portugal's economic policies and strategies as it navigates the complexities of the European and global economic landscape. As Portugal moves forward, the emphasis on innovation, sustainability, and social inclusivity will be crucial in ensuring that the benefits of recovery are widely shared among its citizens.

Chapter 14

Contemporary Portugal

Portugal in the 21st Century

The 21st century has been a transformative period for Portugal, marked by significant political, economic, and social changes that have reshaped the nation's identity and its role in the global community. In the wake of the Carnation Revolution of 1974, which ended decades of authoritarian rule, Portugal transitioned into a democratic state, paving the way for a modern society influenced by European integration and globalization.

One of the most pivotal moments in recent Portuguese history was the country's entry into the European Union (EU) in 1986. This membership not only provided Portugal with access to substantial development funds but also facilitated the modernization of its infrastructure and economy. The influx of EU resources helped to improve transportation networks, healthcare, and education, allowing Portugal to elevate its living standards significantly. However, the benefits of EU membership also came with challenges, particularly as economic disparities within the union became more pronounced.

The early 2000s were characterized by a buoyant economy, driven in part by the construction boom and the expansion of service industries. However, this growth proved unsustainable, leading to a financial crisis that peaked in 2011. Portugal became the third Eurozone country, after Greece and Ireland, to seek a bailout from the EU and the International Monetary Fund (IMF). The austerity measures that accompanied the bailout were met with widespread public protests, reflecting the social discontent resulting from cuts to public spending, pensions, and wages. This period of economic hardship significantly impacted the Portuguese populace, leading to increased unemployment rates and emigration, particularly among the youth seeking opportunities abroad.

In the years following the crisis, Portugal adopted a series of structural reforms aimed at revitalizing its economy. The government focused on fiscal discipline, improving competitiveness, and promoting exports. By 2014, these efforts began to yield positive results, with Portugal experiencing a return to economic growth. The tourism sector, in particular, emerged as a critical driver of recovery, attracting millions of visitors to cities like Lisbon and Porto, as well as the picturesque Algarve region. This resurgence in tourism not only bolstered the economy but also reinvigorated national pride and cultural identity.

The 21st century has also seen Portugal grappling with the complexities of globalization and immigration. The influx of immigrants from various countries has enriched Portuguese culture, leading to a more diverse society. However, it has also prompted discussions around national identity and integration, as Portugal seeks to balance its historical legacy with contemporary realities.

In recent years, Portugal has positioned itself as a leader in environmental sustainability and technological innovation. The country has made significant strides in renewable energy, with a substantial portion of its electricity now generated from wind, solar, and hydroelectric sources. Initiatives promoting sustainable tourism and urban development are also gaining momentum, reflecting a broader commitment to environmental stewardship.

Socially, Portugal has witnessed progressive changes, particularly regarding LGBTQ+ rights. The legalization of same-sex marriage in 2010 and the adoption of anti-discrimination laws demonstrate the nation's commitment to equality and human rights, further aligning it with progressive values within the EU.

Overall, the 21st century has been a period of resilience and renewal for Portugal. While the country has faced significant challenges, its ability to adapt and evolve has underscored its enduring spirit. As Portugal continues to navigate the complexities of modernity, it remains a vibrant nation, contributing to global culture, politics, and sustainable development. The ongoing journey of Portugal reflects not only its rich history but also its aspirations for the future, as it seeks to carve a niche for itself on the world stage.

The Evolution of Portuguese Culture

The evolution of Portuguese culture in the 21st century is a dynamic tapestry woven from historical influences, regional diversity, and contemporary global interactions. As Portugal transitioned from the shadows of its colonial past and the rigid structures of authoritarian rule, it embarked on a cultural renaissance characterized by innovation, creativity, and a resurgence of national identity.

One of the most significant developments in modern Portuguese culture is the revival and reinvention of traditional art forms. Fado, a mournful genre of music that expresses the soul of Portugal, has gained international recognition as a UNESCO Intangible Cultural Heritage. Contemporary Fado singers such as Mariza and Ana Moura have revitalized the genre, blending it with modern musical elements, thereby appealing to younger audiences while preserving its melancholic essence. This fusion of old and new is emblematic of a broader cultural trend, where traditional practices are reinterpreted for contemporary sensibilities.

The visual arts have also flourished in recent years, with Portuguese artists gaining prominence on the global stage. Artists like Joana Vasconcelos, whose large-scale installations often incorporate traditional Portuguese crafts, challenge and redefine cultural narratives. Her work, which combines contemporary themes with traditional motifs, exemplifies the dialogue between Portugal's rich heritage and modern artistic expression. Additionally, the rise of street art in cities like Lisbon has transformed urban spaces into canvases for social commentary, reflecting pressing issues such as migration, inequality, and environmental concerns.

Literature remains a cornerstone of Portuguese cultural identity, with a vibrant scene that continues to evolve. Contemporary authors such as Gonçalo Tavares and Lídia Jorge explore themes of memory, identity, and the complexities of modern life, often drawing on Portugal's tumultuous history. The resurgence of interest in the works of classic authors, such as Fernando Pessoa, alongside new literary voices, demonstrates a cultural landscape that honors its past while engaging with the present.

The culinary arts have undergone a remarkable transformation, showcasing the richness of Portuguese gastronomy. Traditional dishes have been reimagined by innovative chefs who emphasize local ingredients and sustainable practices. The Michelin-starred restaurant scene in cities like Porto and Lisbon illustrates this culinary renaissance, where chefs blend traditional flavors with modern techniques, gaining international acclaim. Moreover, the global popularity of Portuguese wines, particularly Vinho Verde and Port, has further solidified Portugal's reputation as a culinary destination.

Culturally, Portugal has embraced its multicultural identity, shaped by waves of immigration and globalization. The influx of communities from former colonies and other countries has enriched the social fabric, introducing new customs, languages, and cuisines. Festivals celebrating diversity, such as the Lisbon Pride Parade and the Festa de Santo António, highlight the integration of different cultural influences, fostering a sense of inclusivity and solidarity.

Portugal's contemporary identity is also shaped by its engagement with pressing global issues, such as climate change and social justice. The country has emerged as a leader in sustainability, investing in renewable energy and eco-tourism, reflecting a growing cultural consciousness regarding environmental stewardship. This commitment to sustainability resonates with younger generations, who increasingly seek to balance modern living with ecological responsibility.

In conclusion, the evolution of Portuguese culture in the 21st century is marked by a vibrant interplay of tradition and innovation, reflecting a society that is both rooted in its history and open to the future. The arts, literature, cuisine, and social movements illustrate a cultural landscape that celebrates diversity, fosters creativity, and continues to redefine what it means to be Portuguese in a globalized world. As Portugal navigates the complexities of contemporary identity, it remains a testament to the resilience and adaptability of its cultural heritage.

Immigration and Demographic Changes in Modern Portugal

Portugal's modern demographic landscape has been significantly shaped by immigration, reflecting both historical patterns and contemporary global shifts. As a country with a rich history of exploration and colonization, Portugal has long been a crossroads for diverse cultures and peoples. In the late 20th and early 21st centuries, immigration has intensified, bringing new dynamics to Portuguese society, economy, and culture.

Historical Context

Portugal's history of emigration—beginning in the Age of Discoveries—set a foundation for its immigration patterns. Many Portuguese emigrated to former colonies in Africa, Asia, and South America, especially during the upheavals of the 20th century. The Carnation Revolution of 1974, which ended the Estado Novo regime, led to mass emigration as political and economic instability drove many to seek better opportunities abroad. However, it also marked the beginning of a new phase in Portugal's immigration story.

Recent Waves of Immigration

The late 20th century saw a shift in immigration patterns as Portugal became a destination for migrants rather than just a country of emigration. Economic opportunities and a relatively stable political environment attracted immigrants from various regions. Notably, in the 1990s and early 2000s, Portugal experienced an influx of immigrants from Eastern Europe, particularly from countries like Ukraine and Moldova, as well as from Africa, especially Cape Verde, Angola, and Mozambique.

This trend continued into the 21st century, with the financial crisis of 2008 further complicating the landscape. The economic downturn led to increased emigration of Portuguese nationals, while simultaneously attracting foreign workers to fill labor shortages in key sectors such as agriculture, construction, and services. This dual trend has created a complex demographic situation where both the outflow and inflow of people have markedly influenced societal structures.

Cultural and Social Impacts

Immigration has profoundly impacted Portuguese culture, contributing to its multicultural identity. The presence of diverse communities has enriched Portuguese society, introducing new languages, culinary traditions, and cultural practices. For instance, the integration of Brazilian culture has been particularly evident in the arts, music, and gastronomy, leading to a vibrant fusion that reflects both Portuguese and Brazilian influences.

Moreover, the increasing diversity has prompted discussions about multiculturalism, identity, and social cohesion. While many immigrants have successfully integrated, challenges remain regarding social acceptance, economic inequality, and access to public services. The rise of anti-immigrant sentiment in various parts of Europe has also found echoes in Portugal, albeit to a lesser extent compared to neighboring countries.

Policy Responses and Future Trends

In response to these demographic changes, the Portuguese government has introduced policies aimed at fostering integration and supporting immigrant communities. The National Immigrant Integration Plan, launched in 2010, seeks to promote social inclusion through education, labor market access, and participation in civic life.

Looking to the future, Portugal is likely to continue experiencing demographic shifts influenced by global migration trends. As Europe faces ongoing challenges related to an aging population and labor shortages, Portugal may become increasingly attractive to migrants seeking opportunities in a relatively stable and welcoming environment. Additionally, climate change and geopolitical instability may drive new waves of migration, further shaping Portugal's demographic landscape.

In conclusion, immigration has been a fundamental force in redefining modern Portugal. As the country navigates the complexities of a multicultural society, the interplay of historical legacies and contemporary realities will continue to shape its social fabric, economy, and cultural identity. The ongoing evolution of Portugal's demographic landscape presents both challenges and opportunities, reflecting broader global trends while affirming the country's unique position at the confluence of cultures.

Environmental and Technological Advances

In the 21st century, Portugal has emerged as a notable player in the global dialogue surrounding sustainability and technological innovation. This shift toward environmentally conscious policies and advancements in technology reflects the country's commitment to addressing climate change, promoting renewable energy, and fostering economic growth through innovation.

Renewable Energy Leadership

One of Portugal's most significant achievements in sustainability has been its commitment to renewable energy. By harnessing its natural resources, particularly wind, solar, and hydroelectric power, Portugal has made remarkable strides toward reducing its carbon footprint. As of 2020, renewable energy sources accounted for over 60% of the nation's electricity consumption, a remarkable feat that positioned Portugal among the leaders in Europe for sustainable energy production. The country's investment in wind farms, especially in the northern regions, and large-scale solar installations in the southern Algarve have been crucial to this achievement.

In 2016, Portugal made headlines by running on 100% renewable energy for four consecutive days, showcasing the potential for a sustainable energy future. This success has not only reduced reliance on fossil fuels but has also spurred job creation in green technologies and engineering sectors. The government has implemented supportive policies, such as feed-in tariffs and renewable energy incentives, to promote further investments in clean energy technologies.

Innovations in Technology

On the technological front, Portugal has embraced innovation as a means to drive economic growth and improve quality of life. The Portuguese government has prioritized the development of a digital economy through initiatives that foster entrepreneurship and support startups. Cities like Lisbon and Porto have become hubs for tech innovation, attracting international talent and investment. The emergence of tech incubators and accelerators, such as Startup Lisboa and UPTEC, has provided essential resources and networking opportunities for budding entrepreneurs.

Portugal's tech scene has gained global recognition, particularly in areas such as artificial intelligence, biotechnology, and information technology. The country has fostered a collaborative environment between universities, research institutions, and the private sector, leading to breakthroughs in various fields. The establishment of the Lisbon Council, aimed at promoting innovation and sustainability, exemplifies the commitment to integrating advanced technologies into everyday life.

Sustainable Urban Development

Sustainability has also been a focal point in urban planning and development across Portuguese cities. Initiatives aimed at creating smart cities are gaining traction, with investments in smart transportation systems, energy-efficient buildings, and waste management technologies. The integration of technology into public services enhances efficiency and reduces environmental impact. Lisbon, for example, has adopted smart sensors for traffic management and waste collection, optimizing resource allocation and minimizing pollution.

Moreover, Portugal has actively participated in international agreements aimed at combating climate change, such as the Paris Agreement. The nation has set ambitious targets for reducing greenhouse gas emissions and has committed to achieving carbon neutrality by 2050. Such initiatives reflect a broader understanding of the interconnectedness of environmental health and economic resilience.

Challenges and Future Directions

Despite these advancements, Portugal faces challenges, including the need to balance economic growth with environmental preservation. Water scarcity, particularly in the southern regions, poses risks to agriculture and biodiversity. Ongoing efforts to develop sustainable agricultural practices and water management systems will be crucial in addressing these challenges.

As Portugal continues to navigate the complexities of sustainability and technology, its path forward is marked by a commitment to innovation, environmental stewardship, and social responsibility. The interplay between technological advancement and sustainable practices will not only enhance the quality of life for Portuguese citizens but also position Portugal as a leader in the global movement toward a sustainable future. Through continued investment and collaboration, Portugal can leverage its rich history of exploration and adaptation to meet the demands of a rapidly changing world.

Portugal's Global Influence Today

In the 21st century, Portugal has emerged as a nation that adeptly navigates the complexities of global politics, economy, and culture, leveraging its historical connections and modern innovations. The country's global influence is characterized by its strategic diplomatic relationships, economic initiatives, and vibrant cultural exchanges that reflect its rich heritage and contemporary aspirations.

Political Influence

Portugal's role in international politics has become increasingly significant, particularly within the framework of the European Union (EU). As a founding member of the Eurozone and the Community of Portuguese Language Countries (CPLP), Portugal plays a vital role in promoting cooperation among Portuguese-speaking nations, fostering cultural and economic ties across continents including Africa, South America, and Asia. Portugal's emphasis on diplomacy, conflict resolution, and humanitarian efforts positions it as a mediator in various international disputes, enhancing its reputation as a peace-promoting nation.

Moreover, Portugal has actively engaged in global governance issues, contributing to discussions on climate change, human rights, and sustainable development. The country's participation in international organizations, such as the United Nations, reflects its commitment to multilateralism and global cooperation. Notably, Portugal's presidency of the Council of the European Union in the first half of 2021 underscored its capacity to influence EU policies, particularly in response to the COVID-19 pandemic and the associated economic recovery efforts.

Economic Contributions

Economically, Portugal has made strides in diversifying its economy and enhancing its global presence, particularly in sectors such as renewable energy, technology, and tourism. The government has invested heavily in renewable energy, positioning Portugal as a leader in sustainable practices. By 2020, renewable sources accounted for approximately 60% of the country's electricity generation, showcasing its commitment to environmental sustainability and innovation.

Portugal's burgeoning technology sector, particularly in cities like Lisbon and Porto, has attracted significant foreign investment and talent, making it a burgeoning hub for startups and tech companies. Initiatives such as the Web Summit, which has turned Lisbon into a global technology conference destination, illustrate Portugal's ability to integrate into the international tech ecosystem and foster entrepreneurial growth.

Tourism also remains a cornerstone of Portugal's economy, with the nation being recognized as one of the top travel destinations in the world. The influx of international tourists contributes significantly to the economy while also facilitating cultural exchange, allowing Portugal to share its rich history, cuisine, and artistic traditions with the world.

Cultural Exchange

Culturally, Portugal continues to exert a profound influence globally through its arts, cuisine, and language. The country's music, especially fado, has garnered international acclaim, while its culinary traditions, characterized by a fusion of Mediterranean and Atlantic flavors, have captivated food enthusiasts worldwide. Portuguese literature, art, and cinema also resonate on the global stage, as contemporary authors and filmmakers explore themes of identity, migration, and history that reflect both local and universal experiences.

Furthermore, the Portuguese language remains a significant global asset, spoken by millions across several continents. This linguistic connection fosters cultural ties within the CPLP and promotes cultural diplomacy, enhancing Portugal's influence in formerly colonized nations.

In conclusion, Portugal's global influence today is a testament to its historical legacy and modern adaptations. Through strategic political engagement, economic innovation, and vibrant cultural exchanges, Portugal not only reclaims its place on the world stage but also contributes to the broader narrative of interconnectedness and mutual understanding among nations. As Portugal continues to navigate the complexities of the 21st century, its ability to blend tradition with innovation will be pivotal in shaping its future role in global affairs.

Chapter 15

Reflections on Portugal's History

Lessons from Portugal's Past

The history of Portugal offers a wealth of lessons that resonate beyond its borders and time periods. By examining the evolution of this small nation, we can glean insights into resilience, adaptability, cultural exchange, and the complexities of identity in an ever-changing world.

Resilience in the Face of Adversity

Portugal's journey through history is marked by periods of both triumph and tribulation. From the early struggles against invasions by the Visigoths and Moors to the challenges posed by the Iberian Union and the Napoleonic Wars, the Portuguese demonstrated remarkable resilience. The Restoration War of 1640, which led to the recovery of independence after 60 years under Spanish rule, exemplifies the tenacity of the Portuguese people. This resilience teaches us the importance of determination and solidarity in overcoming challenges, whether they be political, social, or economic.

The Importance of Adaptability

Throughout its history, Portugal has shown an ability to adapt to shifting circumstances. The establishment of a maritime empire during the Age of Discovery required not only bravery but also a keen understanding of navigation, trade, and diplomacy. The Portuguese adapted their cultural practices and societal structures to facilitate exploration and interaction with diverse peoples across Africa, Asia, and the Americas. This adaptability highlights the necessity of flexibility in the face of new opportunities and challenges, encouraging contemporary societies to embrace change and innovation.

Cultural Exchange and Syncretism

Portugal's historical encounters with various cultures—be it through the Romanization of the Iberian Peninsula, the influence of Islamic culture during the Moorish period, or the interactions with indigenous populations during the Age of Discovery—underscore the value of cultural exchange. These encounters led to a rich syncretism evident in Portuguese language, art, architecture, and cuisine. Today, as globalization intensifies cultural interactions, Portugal's past serves as a reminder that diversity can enrich societies, and embracing multiculturalism fosters social cohesion and creativity.

The Complexity of Identity

The history of Portugal is also a narrative of identity formation, influenced by its geographical position, colonial past, and political evolution. The transition from monarchy to republic in the 20th century, followed by the establishment of democracy post-Carnation Revolution, reflects the ongoing negotiation of national identity. This historical context prompts reflection on the complexities of identity in modern societies, where questions of heritage, inclusivity, and belonging are increasingly pertinent. It encourages contemporary nations to engage in dialogues about their identities, recognizing the multifaceted nature of national narratives.

Lessons on Governance and Civil Society

The rise and fall of various regimes in Portuguese history—be it the consolidation of the Estado Novo or the democratic transition following the Carnation Revolution—illustrate the significance of governance and civil society. The fragility of democratic institutions, the dangers of authoritarianism, and the importance of civic engagement are lessons that remain relevant. Portugal's experience emphasizes the need for transparency, accountability, and citizen participation in governance to sustain a healthy democracy.

Environmental Awareness and Sustainable Practices

In contemporary discourse, Portugal's historical relationship with its environment, particularly during the Age of Discovery, reflects the impact of exploitation on natural resources and indigenous cultures. As Portugal navigates modern challenges, such as climate change and sustainability, the lessons from its past regarding stewardship of resources and respect for ecological balance become increasingly crucial.

The Enduring Legacy of the Portuguese Empire

The Portuguese Empire, one of the longest-lived global empires in history, spanned nearly six centuries, from the early 15th century until the mid-20th century. Its legacy is profoundly woven into the fabric of the modern world, influencing various aspects of culture, language, religion, and trade across continents. This enduring legacy can be examined through several key lenses:

linguistic influence, cultural syncretism, religious dissemination, and global trade networks.

Linguistic Influence

One of the most visible legacies of the Portuguese Empire is the widespread use of the Portuguese language. As a result of colonial expansion, Portuguese became the official language in several countries, including Brazil, Angola, Mozambique, Guinea-Bissau, Cape Verde, and São Tomé and Príncipe. Today, Portuguese is the sixth most spoken language in the world, with over 260 million speakers. The language serves not only as a means of communication but also as a vessel for cultural identity. Literature, music, and art produced in Portuguese-speaking countries reflect the diverse influences of the empire while preserving unique local traditions.

Cultural Syncretism

The Portuguese Empire was characterized by a remarkable degree of cultural exchange and syncretism. In regions such as Brazil, the blending of indigenous, African, and Portuguese cultures created unique artistic expressions, culinary traditions, and social practices. For example, Brazilian music genres like samba and bossa nova draw from African rhythms and Portuguese melodic structures. The fusion of these diverse cultural elements is a testament to the enduring impact of colonial interactions and continues to shape local cultures today.

In addition to music, syncretism is evident in religious practices. For instance, the blend of African traditional religions with Catholicism resulted in unique forms of worship, such as Candomblé in Brazil and Vodun in parts of West Africa. These practices reflect the resilience and adaptability of cultural identities, demonstrating how colonial histories can lead to rich, hybrid cultural landscapes.

Religious Dissemination

The Portuguese Empire also played a significant role in the spread of Christianity, particularly Catholicism, across the globe. Missionaries accompanied explorers and settlers, establishing churches and converting local populations. The legacy of this religious dissemination remains evident today, as Catholicism is the predominant religion in many former Portuguese colonies. This religious influence has shaped social norms, festivals, and community structures in these regions, impacting everything from family life to governance.

Global Trade Networks

The establishment of trade routes by the Portuguese laid the groundwork for globalization. The empire facilitated the exchange of goods, ideas, and technologies, connecting Europe, Africa, Asia, and the Americas. The spice trade, in particular, was a significant driver of economic activity, leading to the establishment of a global marketplace. Today, the remnants of these trade networks persist in international commerce, with Portuguese-speaking countries continuing to engage in extensive trade relationships.

Furthermore, the legacy of the Portuguese Empire can be seen in the culinary practices around the world. Dishes like feijoada in Brazil, peri-peri chicken in Mozambique, and the use of spices in Portuguese cuisine highlight the fusion of flavors and ingredients that emerged from centuries of trade and cultural exchange.

The enduring legacy of the Portuguese Empire continues to shape the contemporary world, influencing language, culture, religion, and commerce. This complex interplay of historical narratives and cultural exchanges underscores the significance of Portugal's colonial past, reminding us that history is not merely a series of events but a living tapestry that continues to evolve. As societies navigate the challenges and opportunities of globalization, the lessons learned from Portugal's imperial history remain relevant, offering insights into the dynamics of cultural interaction and identity formation in an interconnected world.

Portugal's Contributions to Global Culture

Portugal, with its rich and diverse history, has made significant contributions to global culture, particularly in the realms of art, literature, and cuisine. These contributions are a testament to the country's historical interactions with various civilizations and its enduring influence on the world stage.

Artistic Influence

Portuguese art, particularly during the Age of Discovery, was marked by a unique blend of indigenous and foreign influences. The Manueline style, a late Gothic architectural style that emerged in the 16th century, is one of the most notable contributions to global architecture. Characterized by intricate maritime motifs and ornate detailing, Manueline architecture can be seen in famous structures such as the Jerónimos Monastery and the Tower of Belém in Lisbon. This style reflects Portugal's seafaring legacy and its connections with the broader world.

In the realm of visual arts, painters like Amadeo de Souza-Cardoso and Paula Rego brought Portuguese perspectives to the international art scene in the 20th century. Their works often explore themes of identity, history, and emotion, contributing to contemporary dialogues in global art. Moreover, the influence of Portuguese azulejos (decorative ceramic tiles) has transcended borders, inspiring artists and architects worldwide, particularly in Brazil and other former colonies where these tiles became integral to local aesthetics.

Literary Heritage

Portuguese literature has also played a pivotal role in shaping global narratives. The works of poets such as Luís de Camões, often regarded as Portugal's national poet, have had lasting influence. His epic poem "Os Lusíadas," which celebrates the country's maritime explorations, is not only a cornerstone of Portuguese literature but also a significant work in the canon of world literature. It highlights themes of adventure, identity, and human experience, resonating with readers across centuries and cultures.

The 20th century saw Portuguese literature expand its reach with authors like Fernando Pessoa, whose modernist poetry and innovative use of heteronyms have captivated readers and scholars alike. Pessoa's exploration of existential themes and fragmented identity reflects broader global literary movements and has inspired writers worldwide. Contemporary authors such as José Saramago, who won the Nobel Prize in Literature in 1998, have further solidified Portugal's literary presence on the global stage. Saramago's unique narrative style and thematic explorations of humanity continue to influence literature and provoke thought across cultures.

Culinary Impact

Portuguese cuisine is another significant aspect of the country's cultural contributions. Known for its bold flavors and diverse ingredients, Portuguese food has influenced and been influenced by the various cultures with which Portugal has interacted throughout its history. The introduction of spices from Asia and Africa during the Age of Exploration transformed Portuguese cuisine, leading to the creation of iconic dishes such as bacalhau (salted cod) and pastéis de nata (custard tarts).

Moreover, the Portuguese diaspora has played a crucial role in spreading culinary traditions globally. Countries like Brazil, Angola, and Mozambique have adopted and adapted Portuguese recipes, creating hybrid cuisines that reflect both heritage and local ingredients. The global popularity of Portuguese wine, particularly Port and Vinho Verde, has also contributed to the country's culinary legacy, showcasing the rich viticultural traditions of the Iberian Peninsula.

In conclusion, Portugal's contributions to global culture in art, literature, and cuisine are profound and multifaceted. The country's unique historical journey has fostered a rich tapestry of cultural expressions that continue to shape and influence the world today. From the architectural splendor of the Manueline style to the literary legacies of Camões and Saramago, and the culinary richness that transcends borders, Portugal's cultural heritage is a vital part of the global narrative, inviting appreciation and exploration by all.

The Future of Portugal

As Portugal navigates the complexities of the 21st century, its future appears to be characterized by a blend of continuity and change, driven by economic, social, and political currents within both Europe and the broader global landscape. The nation's historical resilience, shaped by centuries of exploration, cultural synthesis, and adaptation, positions it uniquely for the challenges and opportunities ahead.

Economic Prospects

In recent years, Portugal has demonstrated considerable economic recovery following the Eurozone crisis, which had significant repercussions for its economy. The country's GDP growth has been bolstered by a thriving tourism sector, which has become a cornerstone of its economy, attracting millions of visitors annually. However, the future will require diversification beyond tourism. Investments in technology, renewable energy, and sustainable practices are essential. Portugal has been making strides in renewable energy, with a commitment to become carbon-neutral by 2050, leveraging its geographical advantages in solar and wind energy. This focus not only positions Portugal as a leader in sustainability but also creates jobs and drives innovation.

Social Dynamics and Demographic Changes

Portugal faces demographic challenges, including an aging population and low birth rates, which could strain public resources and social services. To counteract these trends, the country may need to focus on immigration as a solution to bolster its workforce. Recent policy adjustments have aimed to attract skilled labor, particularly from other European Union nations and countries with historical ties to Portugal, such as Brazil and Angola. Emphasizing multiculturalism and integration will be vital in shaping a cohesive society that benefits from diverse perspectives and skills.

Political Landscape and European Integration
Politically, Portugal has been a stable democracy, but its future will likely be influenced by the broader movements within the European Union. As EU dynamics shift with rising populism and nationalism in various member states, Portugal is positioned to advocate for deeper integration and solidarity. Its historical ties to Africa, South America, and Asia provide it a unique perspective on global issues, such as migration, climate change, and economic disparities. Portugal can play a critical role in fostering dialogue and collaboration among nations, particularly in post-colonial contexts.

Cultural Influence and Global Engagement
Culturally, Portugal continues to evolve while celebrating its rich heritage. The global diaspora of Portuguese communities contributes to a dynamic cultural exchange that can enhance Portugal's influence abroad. The popularity of Portuguese cuisine, music (notably Fado), and art has been on the rise internationally, which can be harnessed to strengthen Portugal's cultural diplomacy. As the country embraces its identity, it can also champion issues such as social justice, environmental sustainability, and human rights on the global stage.

Technological Innovation and Education
Portugal's investment in education and technology will be crucial for its future. The emergence of tech hubs, particularly in cities like Lisbon and Porto, signifies a growing emphasis on innovation and entrepreneurship. Encouraging STEM (science, technology, engineering, and mathematics) education will prepare the youth for a competitive global market. The government's support for startups and tech initiatives can position Portugal as a leader in the digital economy.

In summary, the future of Portugal lies at the intersection of its historical legacy and contemporary challenges. By fostering economic diversification, embracing demographic change, advocating for European solidarity, enhancing its cultural influence, and investing in education and technology, Portugal can carve out a resilient and influential role in Europe and the world. As it navigates these uncharted waters, Portugal's ability to adapt and innovate will be paramount in shaping a prosperous future. The lessons from its past will continue to inform its journey, providing a strong foundation upon which to build.

Final Thoughts and Conclusion

The history of Portugal is a rich tapestry woven with threads of exploration, cultural exchange, conflict, and resilience. From its prehistoric roots to its role as a significant global player during the Age of Discovery, Portugal's journey reflects the complexities of human civilization. The nation has navigated through periods of great expansion and profound decline, adapting to changes both internally and externally while maintaining a unique identity.

Throughout its early history, Portugal was shaped by various influences, including the Celts, Romans, and Moors, each contributing to the cultural and social fabric of the region. The integration of Roman infrastructure and the subsequent rise of the Christian Reconquest laid the groundwork for the emergence of a distinct Portuguese identity, culminating in the establishment of the monarchy under Afonso I. This period marked the beginning of Portugal's transformation into a sovereign entity, asserting its independence and expanding its territory amidst a backdrop of neighboring kingdoms.

The Age of Discovery heralded Portugal's zenith as a maritime empire, with explorers like Vasco da Gama opening new trade routes and establishing a global presence. This era not only enriched Portugal economically through the spice trade but also facilitated cultural exchanges that would have lasting impacts on both Portugal and its colonies. However, with great power came challenges; the decline of the empire was precipitated by a combination of internal strife, external pressures, and the eventual loss of Brazil—once its most lucrative colony.

The subsequent Iberian Union and the Restoration War highlight Portugal's resilience as it fought to reclaim its independence and sovereignty. The Pombaline Era introduced significant reforms, showcasing the nation's ability to modernize and adapt in the wake of challenges, notably the devastating earthquake of 1755. However, the 19th and 20th centuries presented new trials, from the instability of the First Republic to the authoritarian Estado Novo regime. Each phase of this tumultuous history reflects the tensions between tradition and modernity, freedom and repression.

The Carnation Revolution of 1974 was a pivotal moment that not only led to the end of the Estado Novo but also laid the foundation for a democratic society. This transition marked a significant shift towards civil liberties and political participation, aligning Portugal with broader European democratic trends. The subsequent accession to the European Union in 1986 further integrated Portugal into a larger political and economic framework, providing opportunities for growth while also presenting new challenges, such as the Eurozone crisis.

As we reflect on the journey through Portugal's history, it becomes evident that the nation is a testament to resilience and adaptability. The lessons gleaned from its past—particularly the importance of collaboration, cultural exchange, and the ability to learn from adversity—are invaluable as Portugal navigates the complexities of the 21st century. The evolution of Portuguese culture, demographic changes due to immigration, and advancements in sustainability and technology signal a nation that is not only aware of its historical baggage but is also committed to forging a progressive future.

In conclusion, Portugal's history is not merely a chronicle of events but a narrative filled with lessons about identity, resilience, and adaptation. As the country continues to evolve within the European context and on the global stage, it carries with it the rich legacy of its past while embracing the challenges and opportunities that lie ahead. The future of Portugal will undoubtedly be shaped by its historical experiences, cultural richness, and its ongoing quest for a balanced identity in an interconnected world.

Help Us Share Your Thoughts!

Dear reader,

Thank you for spending your time with this book. We hope it brought you enjoyment and a few new ideas to think about. If there was anything that didn't work for you, or if you have suggestions on how we can improve, please let us know at **kontakt@skriuwer.com**. Your feedback means a lot to us and helps us make our books even better.

If you enjoyed this book, we would be very grateful if you left a review on the site where you purchased it. Your review not only helps other readers find our books, but also encourages us to keep creating more stories and materials that you'll love.

By choosing Skriuwer, you're also supporting **Frisian**—a minority language mainly spoken in the northern Netherlands. Although **Frisian** has a rich history, the number of speakers is shrinking, and it's at risk of dying out. Your purchase helps fund resources to preserve and promote this language, such as educational programs and learning tools. If you'd like to learn more about Frisian or even start learning it yourself, please visit **www.learnfrisian.com**.

Thank you for being part of our community. We look forward to sharing more books with you in the future.

Warm regards,
The Skriuwer Team

Printed in Great Britain
by Amazon

60957673R00080